Volume 14

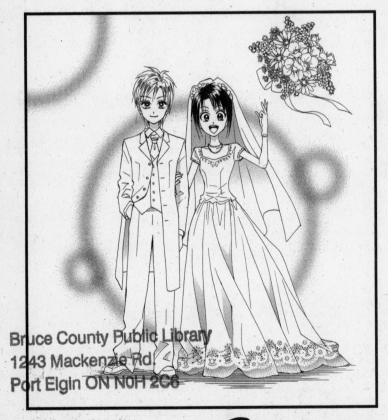

Story & Art by Emura

W Juliet
Volume 14

Story and Art by Emura

Translation & English Adaptation/Naomi Kokubo & Jeff Carlson
Touch-up Art & Lettering/Krysta Lau, Imaginary Friends Studios
Design/Hidemi Sahara
Editor/Carrie Shepherd

Managing Editor/Megan Bates
Editorial Director/Elizabeth Kawasaki
Editor in Chief/Alvin Lu
Sr. Director of Acquisitions/Rika Inouye
Sr. VP of Marketing/Liza Coppola
Exec. VP of Sales & Marketing/John Easum
Publisher/Hyoe Narita

Printed in the U.S.A.

Published by VIZ Media, LLC
P.O. Box 77010
San Francisco, CA 94107

10 9 8 7 6 5 4 3 2 1
First printing, January 2007

www.viz.com
store.viz.com

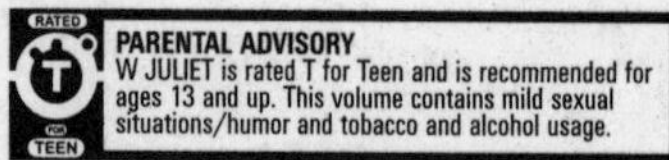

W Juliet

↑ 2002 Hana to Yume No. 23 splash page, draft (B5 size), final episode

↓ 2003 Hana to Yume No. 3 splash page, draft (B5 size)

—Behind the Scenes Story ①—

Ito's hairstyle received split opinions.

But I really wanted to cut her bangs. I thought of using a hairpin or something, but I realized she'd never do such a thing, and that's how this came about. (Laugh) She uses one soon after she graduates, though.

I hope she looks a little more feminine to you now.

WHAT'S UP WITH ITO-SAN?
IT'S BEEN A WHILE SINCE WE SAW HER...
BUT SHE SEEMS SUPER GRUMPY.
CHATTER
CHATTER
CHATTER
...
MAYBE SHE HATES COMING TO SCHOOL.
THREE DAYS HAVE ALREADY PASSED SINCE THE GRADUATION TRIP.
I'VE BEEN IN A BAD MOOD ALL THAT TIME.
REPLAY
YOU DECEIVED US, YOU JERK!!
EXPLAIN WHAT'S GOING ON, ITO.
MY BROTHER UNEXPECTEDLY DISCOVERED MAKO'S TRUE IDENTITY, AND I PANICKED.
AFTER COMPLETELY FREAKING ME OUT, THIS WAS WHAT I GOT.
GYA HA HA HA! LOOK AT HER FACE!
HE'S LAUGHING, TOO.
THE FACT IS, WHILE I WAS SICK IN BED, THEY LEARNED THE TRUTH AND SETTLED THE MATTER...
JERKS. THEY THOUGHT IT WAS ENTERTAINING TO SEE MY REACTION.
THAT'S WHY I HATE ADULTS!
That's how she found out.
I MEAN, I CAN'T BELIEVE I FELL FOR IT!
I KNOW WE WERE WRONG TO DECEIVE MY BROTHERS, BUT THAT WASN'T NICE!
URRGH
It really scared me!!
AND SO...

NYAAH
HOW COULD YOU DO THAT TO ME?! DON'T YOU REALIZE HOW WORRIED I WAS?
I'M NOT GONNA TALK TO YOU FOR A WHILE.
YOU DESERVE IT!

I'M PUNISHING MAKOTO, THEIR ACCOMPLICE.
ITO-SAN, ISN'T IT ABOUT TIME YOU STOP BEING UPSET?
TMP
TMP
TMP

BUT WOULDN'T THIS CONVER-SATION COUNT?
Feels Like déjà vu...
IT'S ONLY A WEEK BEFORE GRAD-UATION.
SILENCE
WE WON'T BE AT SCHOOL UNTIL THE DAY BEFORE.
SNUB
AND I WON'T BE SEEING YOU FOR A WHILE.
HUH ?!

HOLD ON! WHAT'S THAT ABOUT?
OOPS. SORRY. YOU'RE NOT TALKING TO ME, RIGHT?
YOU JERK!
IF I CAN'T SEE YOU, THAT'S A TOTALLY DIFFERENT STORY.

MAKOTO ALWAYS WINS IN THE END.
YOU'RE GONNA GET A JOB?
YUP. I ACTUALLY WANTED TO START AT THE BEGINNING OF THIS MONTH, BUT BECAUSE OF THE AUDITION, I DIDN'T.
COME APRIL, WE'LL BE ATTENDING THE TRAINING SCHOOL, SO I'D BETTER SAVE SOME MONEY NOW.
BUT WHY THE RUSH? CAN'T YOU WAIT UNTIL YOU GRADUATE?
WELL...
I JUST WANT TO REACH MY GOAL SOONER.
?
BY THE WAY... IS IT OKAY TO LET ME IN YOUR HOUSE?
DON'T WORRY. RYŪYA WANTS ME TO BRING YOU HERE RATHER THAN HAVE ME GO TO YOUR APARTMENT.
Theater
BUT WHEN ARE YOU GONNA START WORKING?
KACHAK

GREETINGS

Hello! This is Emura.

At long last, it's WJ's final volume.

I hope you'll enjoy it through to the end.

As a matter of fact, this volume was released on March 19!!

The release date fell on my Birthday the first time after I had 16 comics published.

Including the character book

And not only that, it was for the last volume of my very first series. It's a nice way to commemorate it.

By the way, while I was drafting an original story for this volume, my dog passed away.

He was 15 years old. It was definitely due to old age.

HEY, ITO.

I BROUGHT SOME TEA AND COOKIES.

OH, THANKS!

CHNK

HELLO.

HOW ARE YOU?

Well... WE DECIDED TO TREAT YOU THE WAY WE ALWAYS DID IN THIS HOUSE. SO RELAX.

DON'T WORRY ABOUT ME OR YÛTO. JUST ENJOY YOURSELF.

THANK YOU VERY MUCH.

NII-CHAN*?
OH, DON'T WORRY.
AFTER I EAT THE COOKIES, I'LL GO.
MUNCH
MUNCH
SINCE THAT TRIP...

*BIG BROTHER

NII-CHAN'S ATTITUDE APPEARS AS NORMAL AS EVER ...

...BUT HIS BEHAVIOR IS A BIT OUT OF WHACK.

HE BECAME A BIGGER WORRYWART.

I CAN'T HELP RESPONDING TO HIS BEHAVIOR, AND AS A RESULT...

...

...

...

AWKWARD!!
DOOOM
... THIS KIND OF SITUATION CONTINUED.

SEE YOU.
SEE YA...
HE'S HERE

FEB. 21ST, 7:30 P.M.
AND THINGS TURNED FROM BAD TO WORSE.

HUH?
I'M FORBIDDEN TO SEE MAKOTO UNTIL GRADUATION?!
AND YOU WERE ACTING SO SWEET UP TILL NOW!
DON'T BE RIDICULOUS!
WHATEVER! JUST DO WHAT I TELL YOU!

WHAT'S THAT SUPPOSED TO MEAN?! THAT'S TOO WEIRD!
MAKOTO-SAN'S GONNA BE BUSY WITH HIS JOB.
IT'S ONLY FOR ABOUT A WEEK ANYWAY. JUST BE PATIENT.

TMP
OH, SOME-THING SMELLS YUMMY.
TMP
Dinner time
WHAT? ARE YOU FIGHTING?
...

DINNER
OVER
WHAT'S WRONG? YOU WERE MORE NORMAL THREE DAYS AGO.
For sure
CHNK CHNK
SORRY. THINGS JUST BOTHER ME.
WHAT THINGS?

ONCE THEY GRADUATE THEY'LL JOIN THE ADULT WORLD, AND I WON'T SAY ANYTHING.

BUT RIGHT NOW, ITO IS STILL A STUDENT.

CRMBL

I DID ACCEPT THEIR RELATIONSHIP.

BUT WHAT IF THEY ONLY THINK THEY'RE IN LOVE BECAUSE IT'S FORBIDDEN?

THAT'S WHY I WANT THEM TO HAVE A COOLING PERIOD TO THINK ABOUT EACH OTHER.

SOUNDS TO ME LIKE YOU'RE ACTING JEALOUS.

Are you her dad?

NO! I'M SAYING THIS FOR ITO'S SAKE.

AND I WILL FIND OUT WHETHER THEIR LOVE IS REAL!!

BA

DUM

ENSURING MY SISTER'S HAPPINESS IS MY DUTY.

This guy is weird.

I THINK WE ALREADY FOUND OUT DURING THE TRIP.

SHE'S STILL A KID!

IT'S A GOOD OPPORTUNITY FOR ITO TO THINK ABOUT HER FUTURE.

GEEZ ...

MAYBE IT'S YOU WHO NEEDS TO THINK ABOUT YOURSELF ...

... RYÛYA.

RNNNG

RNNNG

WHAT THE HECK! I CAN'T SEE HIM UNTIL GRADUATION?
THAT'S SOMETHING MAKOTO AND I SHOULD DECIDE.
I'M GONNA SEE HIM EVERY DAY STARTING TOMORROW!
Definitely!
PIP
HELLO?

HEY, MAKO? I'M SORRY WE COULDN'T TALK MUCH WHEN YOU TOOK THE TROUBLE TO VISIT.
THAT'S OKAY. I WAS ABOUT TO GIVE YOU A CALL, TOO.
REALLY?

I START WORK TOMORROW, BUT THE THING IS, I'VE GOT TWO JOBS.
AND I'LL BE TOTALLY BOOKED FROM THE MORNING UNTIL 10 P.M.

SO I MEANT TO TELL YOU I WON'T BE ABLE TO SEE YOU FOR A WHILE...

ITO-SAN, ARE YOU LISTENING?

...

She's already regretting the three days she was upset

I'M SORRY.

IT'S OKAY. I'M ACTUALLY FORBIDDEN TO SEE YOU UNTIL GRADUATION ANYWAY.

I SHOULD'VE FORGIVEN HIM RIGHT AWAY!!

REALLY?

I DON'T UNDERSTAND WHY.

BUT... OH WELL... IT WORKS OUT WITH YOUR JOB AND ALL.

CAN'T BE HELPED, I GUESS.

NOPE, IT CAN'T.

NO...

NO...

...

RYÛYA, TAKE A BATH!
OKAY.
BUT I DON'T WANT OUR SCHOOL DAYS TO END LIKE THIS.
LET'S GET TOGETHER ANYWAY!!
?!
NII-CHAN ALWAYS TAKES A BATH AROUND 11 P.M.
I'M SURE I CAN GET OUT IF I WANT TO!
LET'S MEET AT THE BEACH TOMORROW NIGHT AND THE NEXT NIGHT TOO. SAME TIME. SAME PLACE!
BUT ITO-SAN, DIDN'T YOUR BROTHER TELL YOU NOT TO?
AS A GUY, I CAN'T ASK YOU OUT SO LATE EITHER.
IT'S OKAY! IT'S ME WHO'S GOING OUT!
EVEN IF YOU WON'T COME, I'M GONNA BE THERE.

Ha ha
ITO-SAN.
UNLESS I COME, IT'S MEANINGLESS.
THAT'S HOW I GOT TO SEE MAKOTO...
22ND, 11:00 P.M.
...FOR AN HOUR...
...EVERY NIGHT FOR A WEEK IN SECRET.
I CAN SEE WHY NII-CHAN IS WORRIED, BUT...
KACHAK
GOOD NIGHT, ITO.
YOU SHOULD GO TO BED SOON, TOO.
OKAY.
P-TUM

12:30 A.M.
WHOOO
GOOD.
AS LONG AS I GET BACK BY NOW, I WON'T BE IN TROUBLE.
It was close
RATTLE
I WANT HIM TO KNOW HOW SERIOUS WE ARE.
OUR DREAM TO BE ACTORS, OUR WISH AND EVERYTHING...
I JUST WANT US TO MOVE FORWARD TOGETHER.
24TH, 11:30 P.M.
ITO-SAN, ARE YOU GOING TO WEAR OUR SCHOOL UNIFORM FOR THE GRADUATION CEREMONY?

SHUUSH
HUH? I ALWAYS WEAR IT, DON'T I?
I MEAN, NOT THE GUYS' UNIFORM.
OH.
WHY DON'T YOU PUT ON A SKIRT FOR THE OCCASION?
YOU KNOW, I'D LOVE TO SEE YOU IN IT.
YOU...
UM... IT'S NOT LIKE I HAVE A PROBLEM WITH IT. NOT ANYMORE.
BUT I'VE BEEN LOOKING LIKE A GUY THE WHOLE TIME. IT'S KINDA WEIRD AT THIS POINT.

I'LL END UP A LAUGHING-STOCK, DON'T YOU THINK?
I DON'T THINK SO. YOUR HAIR HAS GROWN A LOT, TOO.
I'M ABSOLUTELY SURE YOU'LL LOOK GREAT.
...
COME TO THINK OF IT, MY BANGS HAVE GOTTEN LONG.

OH WELL. LET'S PRACTICE AGAIN TODAY!
WE'VE GOT SO LITTLE TIME AFTER ALL.
FMBL FMBL
YEAH. LET'S START FROM HERE ...

25TH, 12:10 A.M.
...
STM
STM
STM
...
HEY, YÛTO, WHERE'S ITO?
I DON'T KNOW. SHE'S PROBABLY UPSTAIRS.
NO. I LOOKED IN HER ROOM, BUT SHE WASN'T THERE.
SHE'S NOT DOWN HERE EITHER.
THEN ...
...
NO! DID SHE GO OUT THIS LATE?!
KLTCH
HEY, RYÛYA, CALM DOWN!
HER SHOES ARE HERE, RIGHT?
THAT MAKES NO DIFFERENCE IF SHE'S NOT HERE!!
TMP
TMP
LIEUTENANT, IS IT YOUR BATH TIME?
YUP. I'M GONNA GET WARM IN THE BATH.
LOOK, SHE'S HERE.
YOU! HAVE YOU BEEN HOME THE WHOLE TIME?
ER... YEAH? IN MY ROOM.
?!

LIEUTENANT, YOUR HAND IS A SNOWCONE.
Snowcone?!
YEAH, I'M KINDA CHILLY.
RUB RUB
BAM
STMP
STMP
STMP
RYÛYA?
I...I KNEW IT! SHE WAS OUTSIDE!
This late!
HEY, DON'T DO ANYTHING, RYÛYA. LEAVE HER ALONE.
ITO'S JACKET
MORE THAN ANYTHING, I HATE SNEAKY BEHAVIOR!
BUT IT'S YOUR FAULT.
RIGHT NOW, YOU'RE JUSTIFYING ALL THIS SURVEILLANCE AS BEING A PROTECTIVE BROTHER.
YOU SHOULD CHILL OUT.

SHE'S STILL A KID. I GOTTA --
PROTECT HER?
YOU JUST WANT TO BELIEVE...
...YOUR SISTER STILL NEEDS YOUR HELP.
ITO ISN'T A KID WHO COMES TO TELL US EVERYTHING ANYMORE.
THAT WAS MADE PAINFULLY CLEAR DURING THE TRIP.
THEY'RE THINKING ABOUT THEIR FUTURE A LOT MORE THAN WE THINK.
MAN... HE USED TO BE REALLY HARSH ABOUT ITO'S GUY BEFORE...
SHE'S STILL A KID NO MATTER HOW YOU LOOK AT IT!
B-TUM
HEY!

WHAT'S UP?
WHAT'RE YOU TALKING ABOUT?
SILENCE
...
HM?
OH. YEAH, I TRIMMED MY BANGS.
THEY WERE BOTHERING ME.
WHEN I WAS CUTTING, I THOUGHT I LOOKED LIKE MOM.
Hee hee! It's too short
YEAH... YOU'RE THE SPITTING IMAGE.
YOU LOOK MUCH OLDER.
NII-CHAN ?
PAT
DON'T WORRY.
HE'S STRUGGLING INSIDE RIGHT NOW.

YOU JUST STAY THE WAY YOU ARE.
SOMEDAY, SHE WILL LEAVE AND BE OUT OF MY REACH.
I ALWAYS KNEW SHE WOULD, BUT--

25TH, 11:00 P.M.
MAKO!
AS I THOUGHT, SHE WAS OUT DURING MY BATH HOUR.
WHOOO
...
WHAT AM I DOING?
He's hating himself.
BUT WHO KNOWS WHAT'LL HAPPEN THIS LATE.
Peeking uninvited
I'M DOING THIS TO PROTECT ITO!!
←Auto-suggestion
IT'S MY DUTY AS THE ELDEST SON!!
THERE'S A MAN BEHIND ME?!
BABUMP
!!

THAT'S IMPOSSIBLE. WE'RE THE ONLY ONES HERE IN THE WOODS.
BUT I'M SURE I SAW HIM.
I EVEN HEARD HIS FOOT-STEPS.
THERE IT IS AGAIN.
?
WHAT THE HECK? ACTING?
WAS SHE SNEAKING OUT EVERY NIGHT FOR THIS?
I thought they'd be fooling around
COME TO THINK OF IT, I'VE NEVER DONE MYSTERY.
WE ALMOST ALWAYS PLAYED COMEDY AT SCHOOL. IT'S HARD.

I HOPE WE'LL GET TO DO A BUNCH OF DIFFERENT GENRES AFTER WE JOIN THE TROUPE.
舞台
YEAH!
I'D LOVE TO TRY A HEART-WARMING DRAMA AND A MYSTERY.
AND OUR GOAL IS THE DEBUT!!

MIYABI TENDS TO DO MORE ACTION PLAYS.
AND THERE AREN'T MANY PEOPLE WHO ARE AS ATHLETIC AS YOU ARE, ITO-SAN. I HAVE NO DOUBT YOU'LL GET TO PERFORM.
Miyabi is the theater troupe's name.
RIGHT BACK AT YOU.
BUT... COME MARCH, I'D BETTER FIND A JOB.
GOTTA PAY FOR MY BOARD AT HOME.

ONCE WE GRADUATE, WE'RE OFFICIALLY GROWN-UPS.
I CAN'T DEPEND ON MY DAD AND BROTHERS FOREVER.
I'D BETTER WORK JUST AS HARD AS YOU, MAKO.
WHETHER IT'S THE JOB, THE SCHOOL OR THE TROUPE!
AND WE'LL MAKE SURE TO GET TOGETHER LIKE THIS.
Even if we're busy, we'll find the time!
WELL, WE'LL BE TOGETHER AT THE SCHOOL AND IN THE TROUPE.
THAT'S NOT THE POINT!
AND, ITO-SAN, I'LL BE JUST AS BUSY WORKING IN MARCH.
I'm sorry.
I'LL CHANGE JOBS IN APRIL, THOUGH.
WHAAT?!
I'LL HAVE SOME DAYS OFF, TOO.

WHY'RE YOU SAVING SO MUCH ?!
IT'S A SECRET. ♪
TELL ME !
...
"THEY'RE...
"...THINKING ABOUT THEIR FUTURE A LOT MORE THAN WE THINK."
DID YOU FIND OUT WHAT YOU NEEDED TO KNOW?
RYÛYA?
!

You jerk!!
YOU! WASN'T IT YOU WHO TOLD ME TO LEAVE HER ALONE ?!
I JUST FOLLOWED YOU. THAT'S ALL.
SO?
WHAT DO YOU THINK ?
DO YOU STILL FEEL THE SAME WAY ?
DUNNO.
BUT THEY MADE ME FEEL...
... LIKE I'M THE ONE WHO'S A KID.
IT'S ABOUT TIME...
...I ACCEPT THE FACT.

OUR JOB WAS ALREADY FINISHED LONG AGO.

HOW COME RYÛYA'S IN MY ROOM TONIGHT OF ALL NIGHTS?

IT'S BAD. HE'S GONNA BE REALLY MAD!!

DOOOM

...

26TH, 12:10 A.M.

N-NII-CHAN.

UM... I...

What am I gonna do?

What am I gonna do?

ER ...

What am I gonna do?

What am I gonna do?

TOSS

SST

AAHHH!

PAT

YOU'LL ALWAYS BE MY YOUNGER SISTER, AND I HAVE A FEELING I'LL ALWAYS TREAT YOU LIKE A KID.
I WANT YOU TO REMEMBER THAT.
...
HUH?
BUT YOU'VE REALLY GROWN UP, AND YOU'RE A FINE WOMAN NOW.
INTELLECTUALLY, I ACCEPTED MAKOTO-SAN, BUT EMOTIONALLY AND PHYSICALLY, I COULDN'T.
I'M SORRY.
NO ONE HAS THE RIGHT TO RESTRICT YOU, ITO.
YOU CAN GO WHEREVER YOU WANT WHENEVER YOU WANT.

I DIDN'T UNDERSTAND WHY NII-CHAN CHANGED HIS MIND ALL OF A SUDDEN.

JUST DON'T MAKE US WORRY, OKAY?!

BUT HE LOOKED ODDLY HAPPY...

...AND SOMEHOW, THE AWKWARDNESS WAS NO LONGER THERE.

WELL, YOU'VE STILL GOT THE MORE DIFFICULT ONE--DAD--TO DEAL WITH.

YOU STILL HAVE BIG TROUBLE AHEAD, ITO.

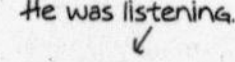

He was listening.

THAT'S RIGHT! I'VE GOT TO INTRODUCE HIM ONCE WE GRADUATE!
WHAT SHOULD I DO, YÛTO?!
DON'T ASK ME.

I'D LOVE TO HELP YOU OUT...
...BUT THIS IS SOMETHING YOU TWO SHOULD OVERCOME TOGETHER.
BUT...
I'M SURE YOU TWO COULD EVEN CRUSH A ROCK AS LONG AS YOUR FAITH IS STRONG ENOUGH.

!!
YOU CAN'T DEPEND ON US FOREVER, RIGHT?
ONCE YOU GRADUATE, YOU'RE OFFICIALLY ADULTS.
Something's weird here
WHAT'S THAT SUPPOSED TO MEAN?

IT'S EASY...
WHAM
WHOA.
HEY, WHAT'S GOING ON?
STMP
STMP
STMP
NO WAY! WERE YOU LISTENING?!

...TO BE PROTECTED BY YOUR FAMILY.
BUT THEN, NOTHING WILL CHANGE THAT WAY.
THAT'S WHY WE ALL TAKE OUR OWN PATH.

ngrats
to
the
grad

FEB. 28TH 11:30 P.M.

SHUUSH

THE LAST DAY OF SCHOOL IS OVER...

...AND TOMORROW IS GRADUATION DAY.

HAVING FULFILLED HIS FATHER'S CONDITIONS, MAKOTO WILL BE FREE.

BUT I DON'T THINK HE'LL SHOW UP TOMORROW.

BLUNT

...

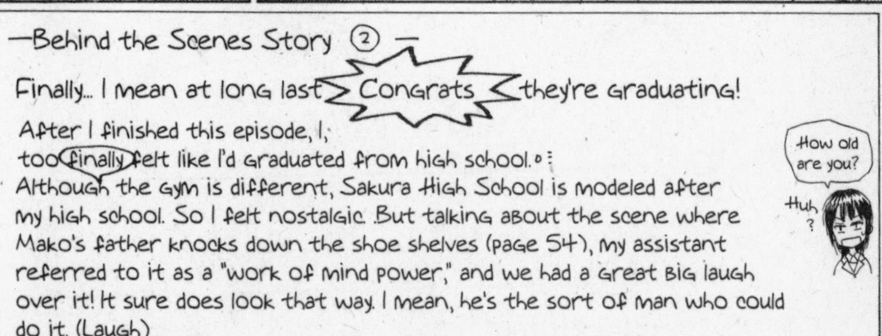

—Behind the Scenes Story ② —

Finally... I mean at long last Congrats they're graduating!

After I finished this episode, I, too finally felt like I'd graduated from high school.

Although the gym is different, Sakura High School is modeled after my high school. So I felt nostalgic. But talking about the scene where Mako's father knocks down the shoe shelves (page 54), my assistant referred to it as a "work of mind power," and we had a great big laugh over it! It sure does look that way. I mean, he's the sort of man who could do it. (Laugh)

SHUUSH
HEY, MAKO, YOU SHOULDN'T BE THAT WAY.
YOU MET EVERY CONDITION AND REACHED YOUR GOAL!
FLIP FLIP
NOW YOU SHOULD FACE YOUR DAD AND MAKE PEACE!
I REALLY DON'T CARE.
WHAT KINDA TIMID ATTITUDE IS THAT?
WHY DO YOU JUST DO NOTHING? YOU SHOULD MAKE THE FIRST MOVE!
I MEAN, GO GET HIM!!
LOOK, ITO-SAN, HE'S NOT MY PREY, OKAY?
NONETHELESS, IT'S THE FATEFUL DAY THAT FATHER AND SON WILL SETTLE THE MATTER.
TWO MONTHS AGO, MAKO'S FATHER PROMISED TO COME TO THE GRADUATION CEREMONY.
I'M SURE THEY BOTH HAVE SOME RESPECT FOR EACH OTHER...
...BUT WHENEVER THEY MEET, THEY FIGHT.
NEITHER GIVES IN. IT'S A COLD WAR.
WELL, IT'S NOT LIKE I WANT THEM TO BE THIS WAY...
I'm proud of you, son.
Father, I look up to you
Too weird.
IF YOU KEEP IT UP, YOU'LL MISS SOMETHING IMPORTANT DOWN THE ROAD, YOU KNOW?

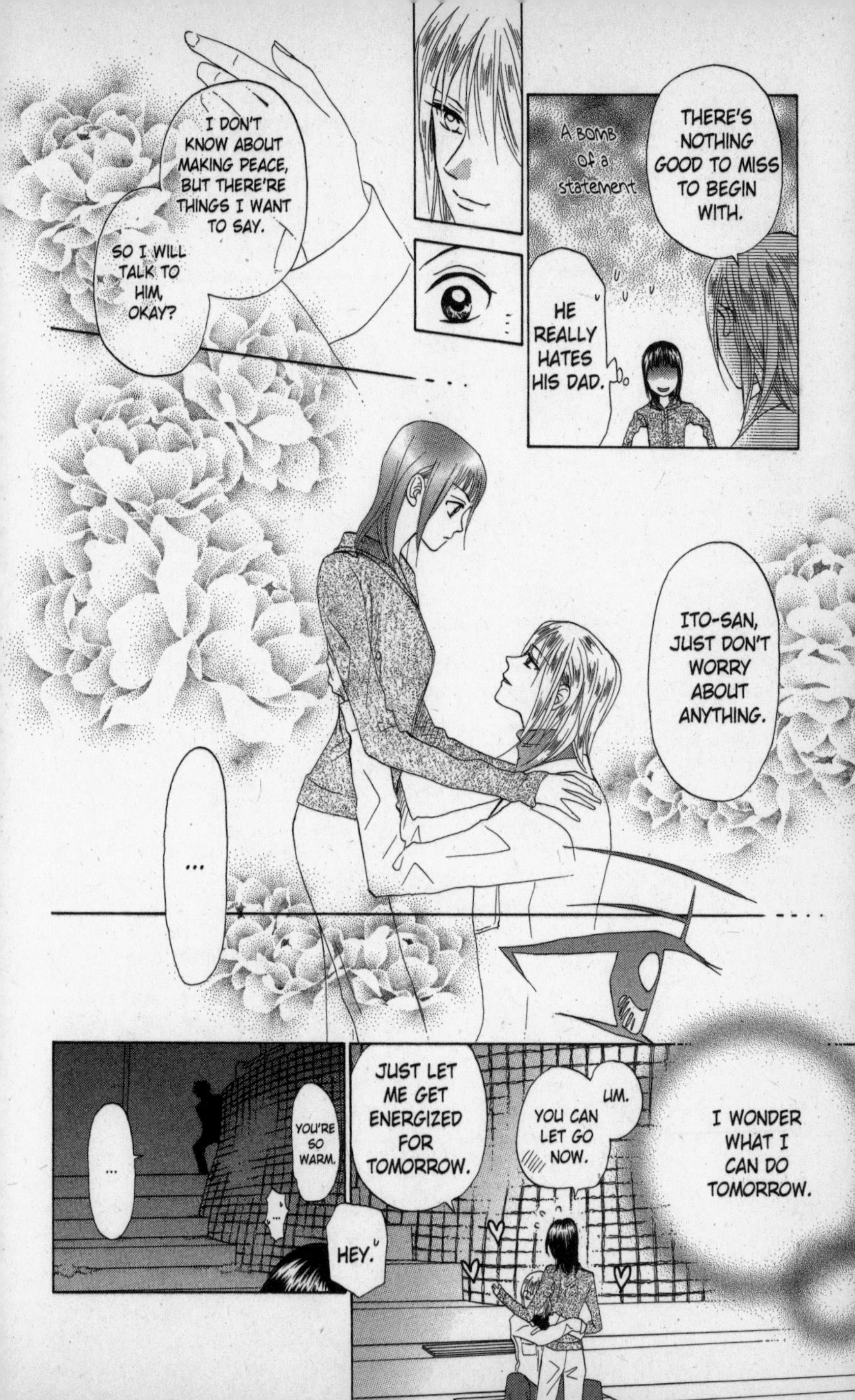
THERE'S NOTHING GOOD TO MISS TO BEGIN WITH.
A bomb of a statement
HE REALLY HATES HIS DAD.
I DON'T KNOW ABOUT MAKING PEACE, BUT THERE'RE THINGS I WANT TO SAY.
SO I WILL TALK TO HIM, OKAY?
ITO-SAN, JUST DON'T WORRY ABOUT ANYTHING.
...
I WONDER WHAT I CAN DO TOMORROW.
UM. YOU CAN LET GO NOW.
JUST LET ME GET ENERGIZED FOR TOMORROW.
YOU'RE SO WARM.
...
HEY.
...

ABOUT MY DOG

My dog that passed away was a female named Chappy. She gave birth to five puppies when she was 3.

↑ Her son, Leo.
Had a mother complex

I kept both mother and son with me, but the mother died naturally this winter on Feb. 3, 2003, and left for the netherworld. She didn't eat for several days, and I knew it was coming.

But when she actually passed away, it was really hard. I stayed in a state of shock, dazed, for a while.

The original story drawn for this volume took the longest time ever to finish.

NO WAY...

IS THAT REALLY MIURA-CHAN?!

SHOCK

WHAT THE HECK? WHILE I HAVEN'T SEEN HER...

SHOCK

...SHE BECAME BEAUTIFUL. HOW DID THAT HAPPEN?

AND THERE'S NO ROOM FOR ME TO GET IN.

DAMMIT! SHE'S STILL DATING HIM!

HOW COME MIURA-CHAN WANTS THAT GUY OVER ME?!

BZZT

BZZT

Whoa! There's this lovey-dovey Barrier!!

!

TMP
TMP
TMP
TMP

?

WHAT'S WRONG, MAKO?

NOTHING... I SENSED SOMEONE NEARBY.

GUESS I IMAGINED IT.

AND...

MARCH 1ST 8:30 A.M.

GRADUATION DAY CAME.

DONNNG

DINNNG

3－2

SILENCE
WH--
WHAT IS IT, GUYS...?
I'M NOT ON DISPLAY!
WOW
ITO-SAN?!
What happened?!
Is that you?!
Beau-tiful!
You look like a Girl
Incred-ible!
What is?
How cute!
SEE? I TOLD YOU IT WOULD BE OKAY.
BUT IT'S WEIRD. I MEAN, THEIR REACTION...
MIURA! YOU FINALLY WORE THE SCHOOL UNIFORM AT THE VERY END!
TEACHER
TOUCHED
I GUESS IT MUST'VE BEEN SOMETHING ELSE AT HOME.
YEAH.
She came sandwiched between her howling dad and bro.
IT WAS QUITE A BIT OF TROUBLE GETTING HERE.
LOOK, THE CHERRY BLOSSOMS ARE ALREADY BLOOMING!
SERIOUSLY?
IT'S WAY TOO SOON!
AH HA HA
I GUESS THE SUDDEN WARM WEATHER DID IT.
EVEN THE CHERRY TREES ARE BLESSING US!

Ah ha ha! NOBUKO, that's a good one!
...
FIFTEEN MINUTES BEFORE THE CEREMONY ...
Please come no matter what!
...
Mako's dad
JUST TO MAKE SURE, I GAVE MAKO'S DAD A CALL THIS MORNING.
6:00 A.M.
B-BMP
B-BMP
I WONDER IF HE'S HERE BY NOW.
OR...
RATTLE
OH.
SAKAMOTO!
G'morning!
HEY, YOU SHOULDN'T BE SO LATE ON GRADUATION DAY.
Ah ha ha
...
HEY, LOOK OVER HERE! MIURA'S WEARING THE SCHOOL UNIFORM!
THIS IS THE LAST DAY TO SEE HER IN IT!
YEAH ...
OKAY ...
DOOOOM

WHAT'S WRONG WITH HIM? UPSET STOMACH?
MURMUR
USUALLY ...
MUMBLE
Miura-chan, you did it for me! ♥
Shut up!!
MUMBLE MUMBLE
YEAH.
SAKAMOTO'S ACTING WEIRD.
MURMUR
GIRLS, GO ASK HIM IF HE'S OKAY.
CLASSROOM 2, COME OUT TO THE HALLWAY.
AND LINE UP IN ALPHABETICAL ORDER.
TEACHER
HEY, GET UP! WE'RE GOING, SAKAMOTO.
SNAP
FORGIVE ME, MIURA-CHAN!
AHHHHH
I'M THE WORST MAN EVER!!
AAHHH..
Outside
...
YES?
JUST IGNORE HIM, MIURA.
HE'S AN IDIOT.
YEAH ...
MAKO-CHAN.

TSUBAKI-SAN?
CHATTER CHATTER
MAKO! WHAT'S UP?
SHE TOLD ME SHE LOOKED IN THE GYM ...
...BUT HE'S NOT THERE.
WHAT?!
NO! THE CEREMONY IS ABOUT TO START!
...
"IF YOU GRADUATE...
...AS A GIRL, I'LL LET YOU DO WHAT YOU WANT."
HE NEVER THOUGHT IT WAS POSSIBLE.
SO HE DOESN'T WANT TO SEE ME GRADUATE.

I PROBABLY MEAN VERY LITTLE TO HIM.
THAT'S ALL.
THAT'S NOT TRUE. I'M SURE!
AWARD
Narita
ITO-SAN?
PIP
PIP
PIP
I'LL GIVE HIM A CALL AGAIN! MAYBE SOMETHING CAME UP.
It takes more than three hours.
Urk
IF HE'S STILL AT HOME, HE'LL NEVER MAKE IT TO THE CEREMONY.
HEY, LINE UP QUICKILY. NO DAWDLING.
FWIP
AH.

CHATTER
CHATTE
HEY!
MY CELL PHONE!
Guys! You all should leave yours in the classroom, too!
I BET YOU WERE SENDING A MESSAGE OR SOMETHING.
I'LL GIVE IT BACK AFTER THE CEREMONY.
AMANO, YOU'RE UP FRONT. MIURA, YOU'RE IN BACK.
BUT MAKO'S DAD SAID HE'D COME...
...TO GRADUATION!
I WANT TO BELIEVE HIM.
Stop, Sakamoto!
STMP STMP STMP
Teacher
I REALLY DO.

I BELIEVE HIM! HE'LL DEFINITELY SHOW UP!!
KLAP
KLAP
KLAP
KLAP
...
B-BMP
B-BMP
B-BMP
B-BMP
HE'S NOT HERE.
B-BMP
B-BMP
I WONDER WHAT HAPPENED. HE'S LATE.
AND THE CEREMONY IS ABOUT TO START.
OH
NO, NOT THEM!!
I'm looking for Mako's dad, right?!
NOW, CLASSROOM 2.

AH...

THIRD YEAR, CLASSROOM 2

KÔTA AKASAKA.

SAKURA-GA-OKA HIGH SCHOOL GRADUATION CEREMONY

YES.

Third Year, Classroom 2

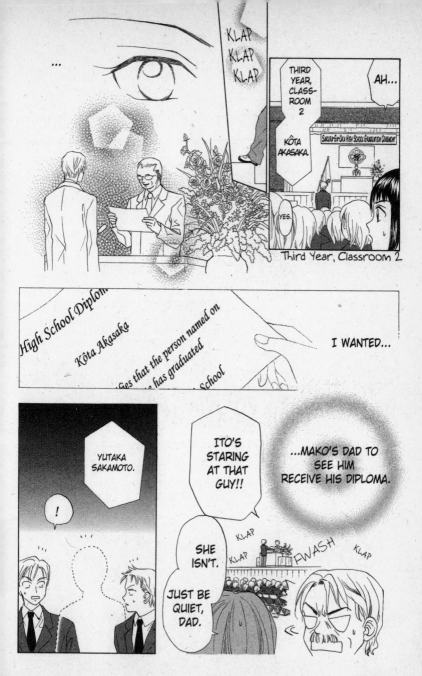

KLAP KLAP KLAP

...

I WANTED...

High School Diplom

Kôta Akasaka

fies that the person named on

has graduated

School

BAM
HE'S NOT EVEN BACK YET.
CHATTER
CHATTER
WHAT?
Seriously?
COME TO THINK OF IT...
EXCUSE ME. LET'S SKIP SAKAMOTO --
?!
MURMUR
MURMUR
WHERE WERE YOU?!
SCHOOL GROUNDS.
I RAN AROUND A BIT TO CLEAR MY HEAD!
HUH?!
KLUTCH
SAKA-MOTO!!
HUFF
HUFF
...
EVERYONE, PLEASE LISTEN!!
RIGHT NOW, I MUST TURN INTO...
...A CRUEL MONSTER SO I CAN SAY THIS!!
SKREECH
?!

MUR MUR
WHAT'S HE GOING TO DO?!
STOP HIM FAST!
FIRST, MIURA-CHAN FROM MY CLASSROOM !!
I KNOW YOU WERE WITH A GUY AT THE BEACH LAST NIGHT!!
NO WAY!
KYAAHHH
SERI-OUSLY ?!
THAT MIURA ?!
WHAAAT?!
HOLD IT...
!!
YOU JERK! WHAT'RE YOU SAYING?!
AND I CAME TO A REALI-ZATION!!
ABOUT MAKOTO-CHAN FROM THE SAME CLASSROOM!

I...
NO WAY.
GULP
IF HE SAW US...
...TOGETH-ER LAST NIGHT...
DOES THAT MEAN HE REALIZED MAKOTO'S A GUY?!
TUNK

KA
BOOOM
WHAT WAS THAT NOISE?!
OH NO! THE SHOE SHELVES AT THE FRONT ENTRANCE ...
SILENCE!
AAHHH
GYAAHH
NOOO
SAKURA-GA-OKA HIGH SCHOOL GRADUATION CERE

...ARE ALL KNOCKED DOWN!!
BA-DOOM
Gak! You serious?!
WOW, it's impossible
HEY, GUYS! I'M NOT DONE --
CHATTER CHATTER
WHAM
STOP RIGHT THERE, YOU JERK!
GET OFF THE STAGE!!
BUT I...I JUST WANTED TO ANNOUNCE THAT I'M GONNA ...
...GIVE YOU UP, MIURA-CHAN, AND GO AFTER MAKOTO-CHAN.
HUH?!
THAT'S ALL...
...
WOOP
HE MADE THIS MUCH RACKET FOR A STUPID REASON LIKE THAT?

OH!
MAKOTO'S MOM AND DAD!!
THOSE SHOE SHELVES... COULD IT BE...?
WHAT?

MAKO'S DAD...

...RESCUED HIM?

ITO-SAN, TAKE A PHOTO WITH ME NEXT. ♡

CHATTER

CHATTER

KYA HA HA

Congrats Graduates!

HUH?

AH, ITO'S ONII-SAN AND DAD, PLEASE JOIN US, TOO. ♡

HA HA HA

Kyaahhh They're so cool! ♡ ♡

IT TEMPORARILY CAME TO A HALT...

...BUT I'M GLAD THE CEREMONY ENDED PROPERLY.

YUP!

ITO.

WE'LL HAVE A TALK ABOUT THAT MAN ONCE WE'RE BACK HOME. KEEP THAT IN MIND.

URRGH.

Onii-san = Nii-san = Big Brother

IF SAKAMOTO DIDN'T START THAT UP...

...WOULD MAKO'S DAD HAVE WATCHED FROM BEHIND THE SHOE SHELVES THE WHOLE TIME?

!

CHATTER

CHATTER

CONGRATU-LATIONS, MAKOTO.

DON'T WORRY ABOUT THE FAMILY BUSINESS.

JUST KEEP ON DOING YOUR BEST.

THANK YOU, MOTHER.

SILENCE

MAKO

...

Dad

Mom

DON'T YOU HAVE ANYTHING TO SAY?

AFTER ALL, YOU'RE THE ONE WHO MADE THE CONDITIONS.

RETURN THIS HAT TO THAT GIRL.

Wow.

She came ← to eavesdrop.

...

AND ...

...A PROMISE IS A PROMISE.

YOU'RE FREE TO DO WHAT YOU WANT.

!

THERE'S NOTHING MORE TO TALK ABOUT.

LET'S GO.

TIK

TIK

HONEY!

I'VE ...

...NEVER LIKED YOU, AND I'LL NEVER...

...FORGIVE WHAT YOU'VE DONE TO ME IN THE PAST.

MAKO ?!

What's he saying?!

BUT ...

EVEN THOUGH I HATE YOU MORE THAN ANYONE ...
YOU'RE ALSO THE ONE I WANT TO BE RESPECTED BY THE MOST.
THAT'S WHY I WON'T LOOK AWAY FROM YOU, FATHER, AND I WANT YOU TO LOOK AT ME, TOO.

IF AND WHEN I GET TO ACT ONSTAGE IN THE FUTURE ...
...I'LL SEND YOU TICKETS FOR THE BEST SEATS.
PLEASE COME AGAIN TOGETHER.
THEY DON'T SAY "CONGRATULATIONS" OR "THANK YOU"...
...TO EACH OTHER.

BUT MAYBE THEY'RE CLOSER THAN ANYONE ELSE...
...AND THEY NEED EACH OTHER MORE THAN ANYONE ELSE.

CHATTER
CHATTER
CHATTER
I GUESS THIS IS THE LAST TIME I'LL SEE YOU IN THE SCHOOL UNIFORM, MAKO.
SAME WITH YOU, ITO-SAN.
BY THE WAY, YOU GOT TALLER, DIDN'T YOU?
I WAS TALLER THAN YOU AT FIRST, YOU KNOW.

WHERE'S YOUR FAMILY?
ER... I ASKED THEM TO GO HOME BEFORE ME.
THANKS TO SAKAMOTO, IT'S GONNA BE COMPLICATED.
MUMBLE MUMBLE

YEAH.
BUT WE'LL ALWAYS HAVE OUR DAYS HERE AT SCHOOL...
...AND ABOVE ALL, I'VE GOT YOU, ITO-SAN. WE'LL BE OKAY.
I'LL COME VISIT THEM SOON.

COME TO THINK OF IT, A LOT HAPPENED HERE.
THE JULIET CONTEST.
THE SIGNING ASSEMBLY.
THE SCHOOL EXCURSION.
YUP.
CHRISTMAS.
THE SPORTS TOURNAMENT.
VISITING THE WELFARE INSTITUTION.
JOINT TRAINING CAMP.
THE CULTURAL FESTIVAL.
MAKOTO WAS ALWAYS...
...WITH ME.
TIK

AND...
I WANT TO CONTINUE MAKING MEMORIES TOGETHER.
ALL RIGHT.
NOK
YUP!
ARE YOU READY?
ITO-SAN, OVER HERE!
Let's take a picture together.
TODAY, TOMORROW AND THE DAY AFTER TOMORROW...
WE'LL LOOK BACK AT OUR MEMORIES TOGETHER JUST LIKE WE DO NOW.

...
LATE MARCH
THREE WEEKS AFTER GRADUATION.
RUSTLE
SOON, IT'LL BE THE TWELFTH ANNI-VERSARY...
...SINCE YOU PASSED AWAY.

—Behind the Scenes Story ③—

Mako's short hairstyle received split opinions, too. Actually, there were more who hated it. But I had to give him a haircut to show due respect to his new start! He couldn't have visited Ito's family without having done it. I love short hair myself, and he had it much shorter in the rough draft. But he looked too different, so I settled for the current length.

I know I did it to myself, but it took a long time to get used to drawing him. Oh well.

SNA
TODAY IS THE DAY MAKOTO COMES TO VISIT AS A MAN AT LAST.
SO... ... HE SHOULD BE HERE AROUND 2 P.M.
PLEASE STAY CALM. ALL OF YOU!!
PP
STM
THAT'S AN IMPOSSIBLE REQUEST.
WE'RE GONNA HAVE SOME REAL TROUBLE TODAY.
DOES DAD KNOW HE'S COMING?
IT'S BEEN THREE WEEKS SINCE...
Getting together in secret at night? What the heck?!
NAG NAG
IT'S LONG ENOUGH FOR HIM TO COOL DOWN, SO IT'S PROBABLY A GOOD TIME.
YU
RYU
ITOU
DAD
After Graduation
STM STM
LIEU-TENANT'S HONEY IS COMING?!
YOU SERIOUS? WHAT'S HE LIKE?!
Ah Leave me alone!
I TOLD HIM THREE DAYS AGO.
AND ... ... WHAT'S WITH DAD?
IN FRONT OF MOM'S SHRINE ...
HE'S BEEN LIKE THAT SINCE THIS MORNING.
...
CHINK
DING
!
DONNG

ALL RIGHT! I'M FIRST!!
DASSHH
HEY, GUYS! HOLD IT!!
Towel
CHRIS GONNA WELCOME HIM!!
HE'S HERE...
TMP
TMP
TMP
LET'S SEE... WHAT'LL HAPPEN.
GAK.
WHAMM
BONK
WE JUST GOT HERE. WHAT'S ALL THE NOISE?

"Summer Days," the extra WJ story included in this volume, was drawn in December 2002. If I was drawing it now, the dog might not have been included in the story. Come to think of it, I haven't named him yet. I'd better come up with something!

Talking about the names, I named both Chappy and Ikkei. Apparently, Ikkei came from "Ikkeh!" (meaning "Go!"). (I was 3 years old, and it was a brand-new word I learned.) As for Chappy, I have a feeling I got it from a character I was drawing at the time.

(I was 9 years old, fourth grade.) What a way to name someone!

GRANDMA ?!
HOW COME...?
AND WITH TOMOE AND KOZUE?
?
ZURSSHH
IT'S SPRING BREAK.
NICE TO SEE YOU, ITO-NEE-SAMA!

HANG ON A SEC! YOU NEVER TOLD US YOU WERE COMING TODAY--
HYA HYA
GÔRO CALLED AND TOLD ME THREE DAYS AGO...
... "ITO'S BRINGING A MAN, SO COME CHECK HIM OUT."

WHAT'S THE POINT IN ADDING MORE PEOPLE?
YOU DIDN'T KNOW WE WERE COMING?
BONK
Dammit, Dad !!
I LOVE ITO-NEE-SAMA, TOO!
SO I'VE GOT THE RIGHT TO SEE HIM!

OOPS.
EXCUSE ME.
I'M SORRY. ARE YOU OKAY?
YES.
HUH?
!
WHAT WAS THAT NOISE?
ARE THEY HERE NOW?
STMP STMP
OH.
DAD!

MAKOTO-SAN?!
WHY DID YOU CUT YOUR HAI--
WHAM
YOU BE QUIET.

HOW DO YOU DO? I'M MAKOTO NARITA.
IT'S WAY OVERDUE...
...BUT I'VE COME TO GREET YOU FORMALLY.
JUNK
FA
SSH
RUMBLE
TSSHHHH
TSSHHHH
OH DEAR, IS THAT WHAT HAPPENED?!

HEY, HOW LONG ARE YOU GONNA MOPE, TATSUYOSHI?
YOU HEARD ALL ABOUT IT, DIDN'T YOU?
IT'S NO SURPRISE. HIS IDEAL SISTER TURNED OUT TO BE A GUY.
DON'T SAY ANY MORE!

YEAH...
WHEN I MET YOU LAST YEAR, I HAD MY SUSPICIONS.
MY EYES WEREN'T MISTAKEN!
YOU'VE GOTTEN EVEN MORE FEMININE, ITO.
HYA
HYA
...

BOY
I ADMIRE THAT. ♡
IT'S SO WONDERFUL THAT HE COULD HIDE IT UNTIL HE GRADUATED!!
INDEED. TOMOE, YOU SHOULD FOLLOW HIS EXAMPLE AND ATTEND A GIRLS' HIGH SCHOOL.

LOOK, THAT'S AN ENTIRELY DIFFERENT STORY.

NOW, GORÔ, WILL YOU TURN AROUND AND SAY SOMETHING?!
WHAT HAPPENED TO YOUR USUAL SPIRIT?!
SLAP

...

HE WAS UPSET ONLY A FEW DAYS AGO.
HIS SILENCE SCARES ME MORE!!
BABUMP
WHAT IF...
TUG
...HE REJECTS ...
I'M SORRY WE KEPT IT A SECRET.
BUT I AM SERIOUS ABOUT ITO-SAN.
TURN
DON'T FRET, YOU TWO!!
MAKOTO-SAN, WHAT A TEASE YOU ARE!
YOU GOT ME!!
HA HA HA HA HA HA HA
?!

HA
HA
AHH, THIS IS GREAT.
YÛTO, PREPARE FOR THE PARTY. WE'VE GOT LOTS OF GUESTS TODAY!
HA
HA
WHAT?
ALL RIGHT, WE'LL GO ALL OUT! LET'S ORDER SUSHI!
TATSUYOSHI! GET SOME DRINKS!
WHAT'S UP WITH DAD?!
HE'S REALLY ACTING STRANGE!
THIS IS AN UNEXPECTED REACTION.
BUT I HAVEN'T FINISHED --
NOW, COME HERE EVERYONE!
ORDER WHATEVER YOU WANT!
Sushi
Sushi
HA
HA
HA
HA
...
PARTY
WILD
...

HA
HA
HA
KYAAHH
AH
HA
HA
I'M SORRY, MAKO. YOU COULDN'T TALK TO HIM, EVEN THOUGH THAT'S WHY YOU CAME.
IT'S OKAY. I'LL BE BACK AGAIN.
SEE YOU.
WELL ...
AT LEAST NO PUNCHES WERE THROWN. THAT'S A GOOD THING, ISN'T IT?
PAT
...
NO MATTER HOW WE TRIED...
...HE JUST FOUND WAYS NOT TO LISTEN.
It's a Great night...
...TONIGHT!
SINCE MAKO CAME, DAD...
...AVOIDED OUR EYES.
AH
HA
HA
HA
DID HE REALLY ACCEPT OUR RELATION-SHIP?
TWEE
TWEET
PLEASE DON'T LOOK FOR ME. DAD

WHAT? HE RAN AWAY FROM HOME!
OH DEAR. HE'S TOO OLD FOR THAT...

WHAT DOES HE WANT?!!
GAAHHH
HE PUT UP QUITE A BOLD FRONT YESTERDAY.
BUT ITO, YOU'RE HIS PRECIOUS DAUGHTER AFTER ALL.
HE'S IN A STATE OF SHOCK. SO COWARDLY, THOUGH.
THERE.
NO NEED TO LET HIM TWIST YOU AROUND.
I'M SURE HE'LL COME BACK ONCE HE SETTLES HIS MIND.
?!
YÛTO AND ITO, GO TO WORK!
AND EVERYONE, GET YOUR CHORES DONE!
What?
Oh
GRAND-MA, YOU'RE AWE-SOME.
THIS IS NOTHING NEAR THE HELL THAT COULD'VE BEEN UNLEASHED!
...

RMBL
RMBL
RMBL
WHAAT?!!
NII-CHAN, YOU GUYS KNEW ALL ABOUT MAKOTO-SAN ALREADY?!
I KNEW IT WAS WEIRD FOR YOU GUYS TO BE SO CALM!
!
THAT MEANS... THE GUY WE SAW WHEN WE VISITED THE GRAVE LAST YEAR ...
AND THE GUY WHO SAVED ITO FROM GETTING HIT BY THE BUS...
AND THE MAN WHO PULLED ME AND ITO UP FROM THE CLIFF...
WHO KNOWS HOW FAR AND WIDE THE SECRET WOULD'VE SPREAD IF WE'D TOLD YOU.
WE HAD TO WAIT FOR GRADUATION.
GEEZ.
NOW THAT I THINK ABOUT IT, WE CAME ACROSS MAKOTO-SAN AS A MAN QUITE A BIT.
YOU'RE RIGHT.
HYA HYA HYA
OHHH
IT CONFUSES ME.
GUSH
DISGUISED AS A WOMAN, HE DECEIVED US...
...BUT THE FACT IS HE'S BEEN PROTECTING ITO IN OUR PLACE.
HIS ACTIONS SPEAK CLEARLY.

DAD KNOWS THAT VERY WELL.
MAYBE THAT'S WHY HE ACTED THE WAY HE DID.
PAK PAK PAK
!
You too.
DAD?!
That man in short sleeves!
HEY, NEWBIE!
HURRY UP AND BRING IT OVER HERE.
YOU'RE GOOD, NEE-CHAN!
You should put on your hardhat, though.
STMP STMP STMP
...
HE'S GONE ...
PLIP PLIP
It's raining.

I WONDER WHY DAD LEFT HOME.
IF HE WAS GONNA RUN AWAY...
...WHY DID HE LAUGH LIKE THAT YESTERDAY?
TSSHHHHH
DING
DONG
BADUM
YES, WHO IS IT?!

MAKOTO-SAN?!
MAKO!
WHAT HAPPENED YESTERDAY BOTHERED ME.
AND SINCE MY JOB LET OUT EARLY, I DECIDED TO COME BY.
IS ANYTHING THE MATTER?
SHOGUN LEFT HOME.
HE'S NOT COMING BACK.
WITH THE RAIN AND ALL, WE THOUGHT HE'D BE BACK RIGHT AWAY.
NO, IT'S NOTHING SERIOUS...
I HOPE HE'S NOT PLANNING TO STAY AWAY.
His wallet's missing, too.
ITO, WHEN YOU SAW GORÔ, WHAT WAS HE DOING?
WHAT WAS HE...?
HE WAS JUST WALKING ...
...WITH A BOUQUET IN HIS HAND.
!
IT'S THE ANNIVERSARY OF SATSUKI-SAN'S DEATH NEXT WEEK.
I BET HE'S THERE, IF ANYWHERE.
?

HANG ON A SEC. IT WAS THREE HOURS AGO WHEN I SAW HIM.
WITH THIS WEATHER, HE CAN'T BE STILL THERE.
IS HE A MAN WHO'D BE AFFECTED BY THE WEATHER?
HMPH
...
No, not at all.
I'M NOT DEAD CERTAIN, BUT...
?
RATTLE
WAIT! I'M A PART OF IT, TOO.
ITO-SAN, YOU'RE NOT COMING. IT'S RAINING.
HEY!
I'M THE ONE WHO STARTED THIS.
SO I'LL GO.
WHAT?!
BESIDES, THERE'S ONE THING I HAVE TO TALK TO YOUR FATHER ABOUT.
FOOMF

DON'T WORRY.
I'LL FIND HIM AND BRING HIM BACK.
TSS
H
H
H...
HE'S PRETTY DEPENDABLE, I'D SAY.
MAKOTO-SAN IS ...A GUY AFTER ALL.
HYA HYA HYA
IT'S ABOUT TIME YOU ACCEPTED IT.
WHAT DOES HE HAVE TO TALK ABOUT?
SPLASH

TSSHHHH
Miura Family Tomb

Right on ...

YOU'VE COME ALONE?
!

YES.
...
TSSHHHH

TWENTY-FOUR YEARS AGO...
...WE ELOPED AFTER MY FAMILY REJECTED MY WIFE.
I KNOW YOU'RE PREPARED TO DO THE SAME FROM WHAT YOU SAID A YEAR AGO.
AND YOU TWO SUPPORT EACH OTHER. BY LOOKING BACK, I'VE COME TO REALIZE THAT.
ITO MUST NOT END UP LIKE WE DID.

THAT'S WHY I FAKED SO MUCH LAUGHTER YESTERDAY.
BUT I'M NOT CONVINCED ABOUT ANYTHING YET.
LIKE WHO YOU ARE AS A MAN.
MAKOTO NARITA, 18 YEARS OLD. VIRGO. BLOOD TYPE AB. BORN ON SEPTEMBER 18.
FWASH
WHO CARES ABOUT THAT!!
I'M DATING ...
...ITO-SAN WITH MARRIAGE IN MIND.

I'M NOT HALFHEARTED ABOUT THIS.
JUST LIKE YOU HOLD YOUR WIFE PRECIOUS...
...ITO-SAN IS THE MOST PERFECT BEING IN THE WORLD TO ME.
SHE IS THE ONLY WOMAN FOR ME.
I WANTED YOU TO UNDERSTAND. THAT'S WHY I CAME.
TSSSH
Miura Family Tomb
TSSH
YOU FINALLY MET MY EYES.
!
...
TRUE. I MIGHT HAVE AVOIDED FACING YOU AND TALKING TO YOU.
YOU'VE GOT THE SAME LOOK IN YOUR EYES AS I HAD LONG AGO.
...
Hmm.
I'M GLAD YOU CUT YOUR HAIR.
THERE'S A BIT OF MAKOTO-SAN STILL, BUT...

...THANK GOODNESS YOU LOOK LIKE A DIFFERENT PERSON.
IF YOU'RE SERIOUS, DON'T DODGE ME!
WOOSH
!!

URK...
FSSH
NOW, LISTEN!
IF YOU MAKE ITO UNHAPPY, YOU'LL FIND MY FIST 100 TIMES MORE POWERFUL!
BE PREPARED TO GO TO HELL.
GOT THAT?!
KAFF
...
WITH ...
...YOUR KICK--
FWASSH
DID YOU GET IT OR WHAT?!
HEH
YOUR WORDS HAVE BEEN ENGRAVED INTO MY BRAIN.

SHEESH... NEVER THOUGHT THE DAY WOULD COME SO SOON.
SPASH
SPASH
JUST FOLLOW ME.
ITO WILL HOLD A GRUDGE IF I LEAVE YOU LIKE THAT.
THANK YOU VERY MUCH!
ALL I DID WAS PERMIT YOU TO DATE HER.
YOU'RE NOT GONNA MARRY ANYTIME SOON!
GRRR
GRRR
OF COURSE.
BUT SOMEDAY ...
I WILL MAKE AN OFFICIAL VISIT FOR IT.

SO?
WHAT DID YOU TALK TO DAD ABOUT?
KELLYFIL

NOTHING UNUSUAL.

I CONVINCED HIM TO COME HOME.

HOW DID YOU GET HURT WHEN NOTHING UNUSUAL HAPPENED?

Took a Bath

WELL, THIS IS, SAY, A MAN-TO-MAN PROMISE.

I WAS PREPARED TO SEE BLOOD LONG AGO.

ITO-SAN?

I'M SORRY.
I COULDN'T DO ANYTHING.
THANK YOU, MAKOTO!
DON'T WORRY. I SETTLED THE MATTER WITH YOUR FATHER.
BESIDES, BECAUSE I HAD YOU, ITO-SAN...
I COULD MANAGE TO COME THIS FAR.
I'M THE ONE WHO SHOULD THANK YOU.
SQUEEZE
...
...
Doesn't your bruise hurt?
"SHE IS ..."
!!
Aha ha ha ha ha ha
TICKLE
TICKLE
TICKLE

"...THE ONLY WOMAN FOR ME."
WHEN THE TIME COMES, I'LL TELL YOU WHAT I SAID TO YOUR FATHER.
BUT WILL YOU WAIT JUST A WHILE?

DRIZZLE

CHAT

CHAT

BY THE WAY, GRANDMA, HOW LONG ARE YOU GONNA STAY WITH US?

UNTIL NEXT WEEK.

UNTIL THE ANNIVERSARY OF SATSUKI-SAN'S DEATH.

BESIDES, I HAVE TO CALM HIM DOWN.

Ito's grown up already! Ahhhh

Wahhh

GUNNN—!

OH WELL...

↑Tears

IT LOOKS LIKE THEY GOT OVER THE BIGGEST DIFFICULTY.

I get to meet the Great Madam?!

Her grave, really.

Let's bring a picnic lunch. ♪

NOW THAT DAD OFFICIALLY ACCEPTED HIM...

They became good friends.

LET'S SEE HOW IT'LL ALL WORK OUT.
Hey, what're you doing?
I couldn't help it.
Not a good excuse!
Nope.

TWEET
TWEET
OH?
HOW UNUSUAL FOR ITO TO CLEAN THIS ROOM.
YOU NEVER CLEAN UNLESS IT'S YOUR ROOM.
Whaat?!
AHH, BE QUIET!
TODAY IS THE ANNIVERSARY OF MOM'S DEATH.
THIS IS THE LEAST I COULD DO.

—Behind the Scenes Story ④—

I was so happy to draw Tomoe and Grandma after their long absence.
And the super strong four (page 110). To face them like that would be seriously scary. A howling misery. 0% chance of survival. (Laugh)

Incidentally, due to page limitations, I could touch only a little on Ryûya and Chris. That's why I included a bit more in here. →

Follow me the rest of your life!

Got it! Will do!

Note: Marriage proposal

HEY, SHE'S TOTALLY INTO IT.
LOOK AT HER FACE.
WHAT? ALREADY PREPARING TO MARRY?
WHAT A RESPECT-ABLE LADY SHE'S BECOME!
REMEMBER TO INVITE ME TO YOUR WEDDING!
WHY'RE YOU SAYING THAT? I'M JUST CLEANING.
Why not? Something good happened last week, didn't it?
Yeah! Officially accepted By Dad!!
Urrgh Just shut up!
AREN'T WE ALL GOING TO VISIT MOM'S GRAVE NOW?!
I'VE GOT A LOT TO REPORT, SO I'M DOING THIS!
OH!
RATTLE
RATTLE
SCRUB
SCRUB
COME TO THINK OF IT...
I'VE GOTTA INTRODUCE HER, TOO...
WHATEVER. BUT WILL YOU WIPE A BIT MORE SOFTLY?
YOU MIGHT BREAK SOME--
WHOA
KRRNK
KRUNK
Told ya.
HM?
WHAT'S THIS?

IT SURE IS SATSUKI'S...

BUT THIS IS THE FIRST TIME I'VE SEEN IT.

I DIDN'T KNOW WHAT WAS INSIDE.

WHAT IS IT? A PIN?

LOOKS LIKE A HAIRPIN OF SOME SORT.

A BARRETTE?

MY DAUGHTER IS MY LIFE

MY WIFE

YAH♡ YAH♡ It's so pretty♡

DAD, YOU DON'T KNOW WHAT IT IS?

I'VE SEEN THE BOX MANY TIMES, BUT SHE WOULDN'T LET ME SEE WHAT WAS INSIDE.

MY WIFE IS

MAYBE IT WAS A GIFT FROM A MAN.

Ah ha ha. That's rough!

HEY, DON'T TEASE DAD TOO MUCH.

HE'S STILL RECOVERING FROM THE SHOCK.

MY DAUGHTER IS MY LIFE

GRANDMA, DO YOU KNOW ANYTHING ABOUT IT?

HM?

...

NO... I HAVE NO IDEA.

BY THE WAY, ITO, DO YOU KNOW WHAT THIS FLOWER MEANS?

HUH? ITS MEANING?

YUP.

The son who's left behind, Leo, is already 12 years old himself, so my whole family is worried about him.

He's super energetic and eats tons of food, but since he's been alone he isn't as spirited as he used to be. Perhaps because he's been with his mother, his heart has always been like a boy's.

Apparently, dogs age 14 years in their first year, and we're supposed to add 7 years each year thereafter.

I thought it was 5 years.

That means Leo is already 91, and Chappy was 112 years old! Hers was a peaceful death!

Well done, Chappy.

She loved bread

DUNNO ...
I MEAN, I DON'T EVEN KNOW WHAT FLOWER IT IS.
?
?
HYA HYA
I THOUGHT YOU'D SAY THAT.
WELL, WHY DON'T YOU FIND THE ANSWER TODAY.
?

AND PUT IT ON BEFORE WE GO!
MASTER, THE PREPARATION IS COMPLETE!
LEMME SEE.
HEY! YOU'VE REALLY BECOME A GREAT COOK, CHRIS.
It's our family flavor.
I WORKED HARD EVERY DAY.
WHAT DO YOU THINK? DID I PASS THE TEST, MASTER?

WELL ... I GUESS SO.
KYAAHHH
What're they doing?
I LIKE THAT HAIRSTYLE.
WHAT? REALLY?

MOM USED TO TREASURE IT.
I WONDER WHAT MEANING THE FLOWER HAS.
OH.
HELLO, EVERYONE.
MAKO! AKANE-SAN!
Sure
MY WIFE
THANK YOU FOR INVITING US TODAY.
HEY, YUTO, WHO'S THAT LADY?
SHE'S BEAU-TIFUL. ♥
SHE'S MY GIRL-FRIEND.
SHE'S ALSO MAKOTO-SAN'S SISTER.
I'M AKANE NARITA.
HOW DO YOU DO?
BOTH SIBLINGS GOT HOOKED UP, HUH? GOOD JOB!
AH HA HA HA
ER... IT'S NOT LIKE WE DELIBERATELY PLANNED ANYTHING. IT SORT OF NATURALLY WORKED OUT THIS WAY.
COME TO THINK OF IT, EVERYONE EXCEPT TATSUYOSHI HAS A PARTNER WITH FOREIGN BLOOD.

That, too, wasn't exactly planned for. ﾞﾞ

SO WHAT I'VE GOT NO GIRLFRIEND?

SOMEDAY, WHEN ITO OR YŪTO GETS MARRIED...

...YOU'LL HAVE AN IDEAL SISTER. GOOD DEAL, ISN'T IT?

HMPH

Sister-in-law.

URM?

That's... right!!

LET'S LEAVE THAT IDIOT ALONE AND GO.

He really cares about that

NO!! SHE'S NOT GONNA MARRY YET!!

THAT'S WHY I SAID "SOMEDAY"!

FOOSH

DON'T START A RACKET IN THE GRAVEYARD, YOU FOOLS.

AHH, THE TEA TASTES GOOD.

...

MAN... THEY'RE OUT OF CONTROL.

SURE, HE MIGHT'VE SAID "STAY WITH ME"...

...OR "TOGETHER FOREVER" OR SOMETHING...

BUT I KNOW IT'LL BE A LONG TIME BEFORE HE ACTUALLY PROPOSES.

HMMM

HM?

WHAT?

N— NOTHING!

LET'S JUST GREET MY MOM!

GRIN GRIN

JUST LOOK AWAY! I CAN'T HANDLE IT!
AHHHH
KYAHH
!!
I SAW THIS COMING THE MOMENT I KNEW WHO WAS GOING TO BE HERE.
Totally digressing
I THINK NII-CHAN SHOULD GO FIRST.
AS OUR REPRESENTATIVE !!
YEAH, THE FIRST-BORN.
Missing the point
HEY, DON'T MAKE THAT A RULE!!
Tatsuyoshi, ask Rie-chan to come, too.
I told ya, she's not my girlfriend yet!!
IN-DEED ...
...
THEY'RE CERTAINLY YOUR AND SATSUKI-SAN'S CHILDREN.
YOU SURE WORKED HARD TO RAISE THEM WELL OVER THE PAST 12 YEARS, GORÔ.
THEY ARE ALL HAPPY AND GOOD KIDS.
All right, let's line up!!
"A HAPPY AND FREE FAMILY."
THAT...
...WAS WHAT SHE WANTED.

I'M SURE SATSUKI IS BLESSING THEM FROM ABOVE.
内田家

YOU'RE GONNA GO TO AMERICA?!
RYÛYA?!
Why?!

WHY'RE YOU SO SURPRISED? THAT'S WHERE CHRIS'S FAMILY LIVES.
YUP!
!
ONCE SPRING BREAK IS OVER, THE FLIGHTS WON'T BE AS CROWDED.
WE FIGURE WE'LL BE AWAY FOR ABOUT A WEEK.
WHAT'RE YOU GONNA DO THERE?
WELL ...
YOU KNOW ...
I'M GONNA MARRY MASTER. ♪

WHAAT?!
YOU SERIOUS?!
WHEN DID YOU PLAN THAT?
I'M JUST GONNA GO MEET HER FAMILY THIS TIME!
WE'LL HAVE OUR WEDDING HERE, BUT THAT WON'T HAPPEN FOR A WHILE.
CONGRAT-ULATIONS, CHRIS-SAN!
WOW
K-YAAHH
Awesome! You did it!
HOORAH!!
WHAT ABOUT ME?
...

THAT WAS SUDDEN.
Yû
You didn't tell me any of it.
WELL... ITO'S ORDEAL IS SETTLED NOW.
Ryû
BESIDES, I PROMISED CHRIS...
...ONCE SHE LEARNS TO COOK, YOU KNOW.
GLUG GLUG
?
WE'LL CONTINUE LIVING AT HOME...
...BUT IT'S NOT LIKE YOU'LL DO THE SAME FOREVER, RIGHT?
COLONEL TRAINED CHRIS HANDS ON!
I PASSED TODAY. ♡
Yûto's Recipes
YOU DON'T LOOK IT...
...BUT YOU DO THINK ABOUT THINGS, DON'T YOU?
Ahem
I'M THE FIRSTBORN, AFTER ALL!
He's been in charge of housekeeping.
BUT HAVING YOUR GIRLFRIEND TELL US WAS RIDICULOUS.
BONK
YOU TALK TOO MUCH.
IT WAS CHRIS-SAN WHO PUT TOGETHER OUR PICNIC LUNCH TODAY?
IT'S DELICIOUS!
But it's true!
SHE COULDN'T EVEN FIX PORRIDGE A YEAR AGO.
I think
SHE MUST'VE WORKED REALLY HARD FOR NII-SAMA'S SAKE!
MY DAUGHTER IS MY LIFE.
PUNCH!

...
Got it.
WE'RE ALL WORKING HARD...
...FOR OUR FUTURE.
NOW, LET'S TOAST FOR THEIR NEW START!!
MY WIFE
CHEERS!!
YAY!!
CONGRATULATIONS!!
MIURA FAMILY TOMB
MY DAUGHTER IS
DID YOU HEAR? RYUYA'S DOING IT!!
I HOPE THEY'LL BLESS US LIKE THAT WHEN IT'S OUR TURN.
CHATTER
CHATTER
CHATTER

ALL RIGHT. GIRLS GET THE FOOD.
GUYS WILL GET THE DRINKS.
SEE YOU AT THE CASH REGISTER IN 20 MINUTES.
OKAY!
I'M SORRY. CHRIS IS HALF-BAKED!!
Half-Baked?
NO. IT'S JUST THAT WE EAT A LOT.
IT'S NOT YOUR FAULT WE RAN OUT OF FOOD.
ITO-NEE-SAMA, MAY I BUY SOME SNACKS?
NOTHING MESSY, OKAY?
These three are holding the fort
BUT IS IT OKAY TO HAVE A PARTY AT THE GRAVEYARD?
Hmmm
OH, IT'S DONE QUITE OFTEN, FROM ANCIENT TIMES.
THE REASON SO MUCH LAND IS SET ASIDE FOR GRAVEYARDS IS SO PEOPLE CAN HAVE PICNICS.
Especially in the countryside.
Really?
AKANE-SAN, YOU'RE SO WELL-INFORMED.
PWEET
HEY
I'M JEALOUS THAT YOU ALL HAVE BOY-FRIENDS.
I WISH A COOL PRINCE LIKE ITO-NEE-SAMA'S WILL COME TO ME, TOO.
A PRINCE?!
HE MEANT A MAN.
I'M ALWAYS USED AS A BENCH-MARK.
HMPH, SO YOU'RE FREE THEN?
THAT'S ODD FOR A CUTE GIRL LIKE YOU.
WHAT?
I'm cute?

THEN HOW ABOUT SPENDING THE DAY WITH US?
AWE-SOME. GOOD CATCH.
YOU DID IT!
NO WAY.
CROWDING
?!
OH NO! THIS ISN'T GOOD.
WHAAT? BUT I DON'T SEE... any guys.
NO! WE'RE ALREADY BUSY! THANKS!
LET'S HANG OUT JUST A BIT!
SO CUTE! ARE YOU IN MIDDLE SCHOOL?

YUP. I'M 14 YEARS OLD.
14!
OHHHHH
SO YOUNG!
COME ON! DON'T TALK TO THEM, TOMOE!

I CAN'T PROTECT US AGAINST SO MANY.
GOTTA GET TO THE CASH REGISTER FAST!
PATIENCE
SHE LOOKS NICE, BUT NOT AT ALL SWEET.
HEY, DON'T GO AWAY!
KLUTCH
AHH.

SNAPP
AKANE-SAN. COLONEL'S HONEY!
DON'T! NOT YOU!!
IT'S AGAINST THE LAW!!
WOW, WHAT THE HECK?
SCARY.
DAMMIT. HOW DARE YOU!
YOU BETTER BE PREPARED TO DIE!!
KLUTCH
HM?
?!
WHO NEEDS TO BE...
Is this how to girl hunt or what?
THWACK
...PRE-PARED TO WHAT?
MAKO!!
!
I HEARD THE NOISE, SO I CAME OVER.
ARE YOU WITH THEM?
HEY, YOU OKAY?!
DON'T ACT SO COOL ALONE! DAMN YOU!
LISTEN.

BETTER THINK TWICE ABOUT HUNTING GIRLS TODAY.

What'd you do to my daughter?!
GYAAHHH
KYAHH AAAHHH
BAM
KRAK
SMASH
MASTER, YOU'RE TERRIFIC!!
So cool, all of you, Nii-sama!
AGAINST THE SUPER STRONG FOUR...
I CAN'T HELP BUT PITY THOSE GUYS.
...
MURMUR MURMUR...

HEY! WHAT'S GOING ON?!
OOPS, THE SECURITY GUARD!!
RUSSSHH
SHEESH. DON'T START TROUBLE ON THE ANNIVERSARY OF YOUR MOM'S DEATH!
MY WIFE IS MY LIFE.
LET'S SCATTER FOR NOW.
RUNNING AWAY TOGETHER WILL ATTRACT MORE ATTENTION.
YOU WERE THE WILDEST ONE OF ALL, DAD.
And you're the adult.
HOW COME HE'S SO CLEVER ABOUT IT?
MAKO, WHAT ABOUT THE DRINKS?
ALREADY BOUGHT 'EM. AND YOU?
PER-FECT!
WSSH
YUP!
SEE YA, ITO!
Hey, you punks!
内田
山田家之墓
宮本家
小松家之墓

IT'S ALREADY GETTING LATE.
A DAY ENDS FAST, INDEED.
Miura Family Tomb
PICK UP ALL THE TRASH.
WE'D BETTER CLEAN UP BEFORE WE LEAVE!
TODAY IS THE FIRST TIME GUYS TRIED TO PICK ME UP. ♥
LA LA LA
I'M HAPPY FOR YOU.
DON'T BE HAPPY ABOUT IT!!
HE'S THE TYPE WHO'D WILLINGLY GO ALONG.
BUT HE'S A BOY.
THERE'S A FUNDAMENTAL PROBLEM.
BY THE WAY, ITO, DID YOU FIGURE OUT THE ANSWER FOR THE FLOWER?
HM?

OH, I WAS SO BUSY I FORGOT.
WE'VE DONE A LOT TODAY, YOU KNOW.
ANSWER FOR WHAT FLOWER?
Urm
IT'S ABOUT THIS BARRETTE --

KRAK KA BOOM
I LOST IT?!
ITO-SAN?
I DROPPED IT? BUT WHERE?
WHAT AM I GONNA DO? IT'S MOM'S!!

!
HEY, ITO?!
I'M SORRY. JUST GO HOME AHEAD OF ME!!
WOOSH
I'LL GO AFTER HER!
THANKS.
WHERE?! THE SUPERMARKET?
NO. I DIDN'T GET INTO THE FIGHT TODAY.
ON THE WAY BACK THEN?
IT'S GOTTA BE SOMEWHERE AROUND HERE.
WHAT'S WRONG? WHAT DID YOU LOSE?
YOU KNOW, THE FLOWER-SHAPED HAIRPIN I HAD ON TODAY.
OH, THAT?
WHAT FLOWER WAS IT?
HUH?
...

THAT'S PRECISELY WHAT I DON'T KNOW!!
WHATEVER IT IS, IT'S SILVER, LONG AND NARROW, OKAY?!
GOT IT.
B-BMP
DAMMIT. IT'S NOWHERE.
AND IT'S GETTING DARK.
B-BMP
MAYBE IT'S NOT HERE.
I WAS SO FOCUSED ON GETTING AWAY, I DIDN'T EVEN HEAR IT DROP.
AND IT'S SOMETHING MY MOM USED TO TREASURE!
GLOW

?
OH!
THAT'S IT !!
THANK YOU, MAKO! I'M SO GLAD!!
HOW DID YOU FIND IT?! YOU'RE AWESOME!
!
NO... IT GLOWED ...
I saw it.
HUH? WHAT?
ER... IT'S NOTHING.
LET'S GO BACK.
WHOO

THEY DID GO HOME.
AND I WAS SO SURE THEY'D BE WAITING.
EMPTY
It would've never happened Before
SINCE YOU MADE THE OFFICIAL VISIT, THEY'VE CHANGED.
!
MIURA FAMILY TOMB
IT MEANS THEY ALL TRUST YOU ENOUGH.
THAT MAKES ME HAPPY.
BY THE WAY, ITO-SAN...
WHAT?
...ISN'T THIS A TULIP?
山本家
OH, YOU'RE RIGHT!
I WONDER WHAT IT MEANS.
I KNOW THE BULB IS POISONOUS.
Poisonous...
DO YOU REMEMBER WHAT THAT MEANS?
GLOW
MIURA FAMILY

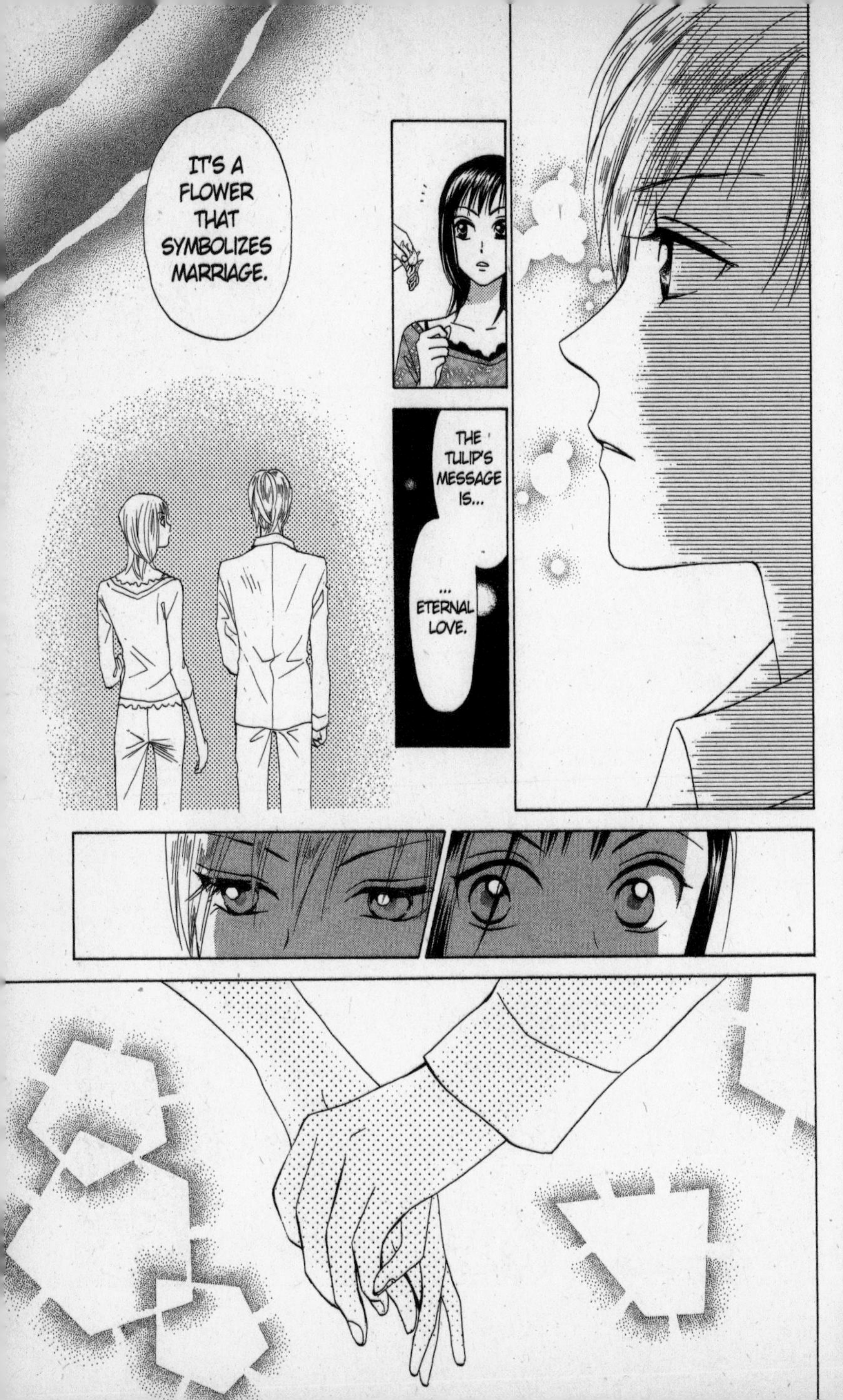
IT'S A FLOWER THAT SYMBOLIZES MARRIAGE.
THE TULIP'S MESSAGE IS...
...ETERNAL LOVE.

WELL ...
?
?
I MEANT TO DO THIS...
...WHEN I BECAME MORE INDEPENDENT.
BUT I HAVE A FEELING I SHOULD SAY IT NOW.
MIURA FAMILY
I HEREBY VOW MY ETERNAL LOVE.
AND SOMEDAY, I WILL COME FOR YOU.

WILL YOU MARRY ME?

WH--
WHAT'S UP WITH YOU ALL OF A SUDDEN ?!
YOU MORON!
Moron
BAM
BAM
BAM
BAM
ER...
THE HAIRPIN SORT OF PROMPTED ME...
!
I NEVER THOUGHT ...
...MAKOTO WOULD SAY SOMETHING LIKE THAT TO ME TODAY.
BECAUSE I DIDN'T EXPECT IT--
ITO-SAN... DON'T CRY.
...

I'M SURE MOM TREASURED IT...
...BECAUSE SHE VOWED ETERNAL LOVE WITH DAD.

THAT'S RIGHT.
THE TULIP'S MESSAGE IS "ETERNAL LOVE."
AND THE TWO OF THEM REPRESENT HUSBAND AND WIFE.
I'M IMPRESSED YOU FIGURED IT OUT, ITO.
IT'S PRETTY MUCH WHAT MAKO TOLD ME...
HYA HYA
I DIDN'T MENTION IT THIS MORNING...
...BUT IT'S SOMETHING I GAVE SATSUKI-SAN AS A GIFT!
YEAH?
GRAND-MA, YOU DID?
YUP.
AFTER I HEARD THEY WERE LEAVING THE MAIN HOUSE TO BE TOGETHER...
I GAVE IT TO HER IN SECRET.

SHE WAS UNFORTUNATE WITH HER PARENTS AND HER SHORT LIFE.
BUT SHE HAD HER SHARE OF THE WARM FAMILY SHE BUILT WITH GORÔ.
YOU CHILDREN PROVE IT BETTER THAN ANYTHING ELSE.
MY WIFE IS
PLEASE TUCK IT AWAY SAFELY UNTIL THE TIME COMES.
TUNK
IT'S YOUR TURN TO FIND HAPPINESS NEXT, ITO.
MY WIFE IS MY LIFE.

ANYWAY, YOU'VE LOOKED CHEERFUL SINCE YOU CAME HOME.
DID SOMETHING GOOD HAPPEN?
HYA HYA
N--
NOTHING IN PARTICULAR
BABUMP
Hey, it's dinner time
WHAT DID YOU TALK ABOUT WITH MAKOTO-SAN?
She knows everything...
DON'T WORRY.
I WILL BE HAPPIER THAN ANYONE ELSE...
...FOR MOM LEFT ME MY LIFE..
I WILL HAVE A HAPPY LIFE.

WE HAD A CHARACTER CONTEST IN THE MAGAZINE TO MEMORIALIZE THE END OF THE WJ SERIES.
THANK YOU VERY MUCH FOR SENDING SO MANY VOTES!
THE EDITORIAL DEPARTMENT COUNTED THEM, BUT ALL THE POSTCARDS ARE WITH ME NOW.
There were lots of comments and requests, too!
ALL RIGHT!
FOR THE BENEFIT OF THOSE WHO READ THE GRAPHIC NOVEL VERSION ONLY, WE INCLUDED THE RESULT.
YOU'LL SEE IT HERE AND THERE IN EXTRA SPACES LIKE THIS ONE. PLEASE ENJOY.
AND WHAT'S YOUR PREDICTION?

...NAL EVENT W JULIET CHARACTER CONTEST

RESULTS ANNOUNCEMENT!!

A CHARACTER CONTEST WAS HELD TO MARK THE ENDING. THANK YOU VERY MUCH FOR SENDING SO MANY VOTES. WHAT PLACE DID YOUR FAVORITE CHARACTER WIN? HERE ARE THE TOP FIVE!

1 ITO MIURA

EMURA: IT MUST BE THE POWER OF THE MAIN CHARACTER. IT GIVES ME IMMEASURABLE PLEASURE. CONGRATULATIONS, ITO!!

MESSAGES: I TRULY RESPECT HER! SHE'S SO GROOVY. / MY LOVE FOR ITO-SAN IS SUPER-DUPER. ♥ / IT'S GREAT THAT SHE'S ALWAYS SO POSITIVE!! ITO-SAN ALWAYS GAVE ME ENCOURAGEMENT.

2 MAKOTO AMANO

...RA: I WAS ...BLE TO ...RAW HIM ...S BOTH A ...OY AND A ...IRL, AND ...T MADE IT ...N FOR ME. HIS ...RSONALITY BECAME ...REASINGLY BOLD AS ...HE STORY ...OGRESSED. ...LAUGH)

MESSAGES: I LOVE HIM SOOO MUCH!! HE MUST LIVE HAPPILY EVER AFTER WITH ITO-SAN!! / MAKOTO-SAN, YOU'RE PERFECT. YOU'RE AN IDEAL MAN. ♥

3 YÛTO MIURA

...MURA: AS I EXPECTED, HE WON ...RD PLACE. ♪ HE MAINTAINED THE MOST POPULAR POSITION AMONG THE THREE BROTHERS ...LL THE WAY THROUGH ...O THE END.

MESSAGES: HE'S SUCH A COOL, MATURE MAN!! / I WISH YÛTO AND AKANE A HAPPY LIFE TOGETHER, TOO. ♥ / HE'S TOO COOL. I LOVE HIM. ♥

4 TATSUYOSHI MIURA

EMURA: HE'S A CHARACTER WHO ALWAYS GOT BEATEN UP, BUT HE ROSE TO THE OCCASION AT THE CRUCIAL TURN. HE'S A SWEET KID.

5 RYÛYA MIURA

EMURA: THE NII-CHAN BURSTING WITH SISTER-COMPLEX!! AMONG THE THREE BROTHERS, I ENJOYED DRAWING HIM THE MOST.

DING DONNNG
HELLO.
HEY.
LONG TIME NO SEE, YOU GUYS!
YOU'RE ALL DRESSED UP. WHAT'S GOING ON?
YEAH.
HA HA HA
IS ITO-SAN HERE?
YEP. SHE'S UPSTAIRS--
CHATTER
STM
STM
STM

—Behind the Scenes Story ⑤—

Because of Mako's proposal in the previous installment, a lot of readers thought this story was going to be about their wedding.

But since the next one after this was about living together unmarried, I couldn't let the wedding take place. Not just yet. Talking about the colored splash page (pp. 126-127), the girls are actually in wedding dresses, and the guys are in tuxedos. The design was so simple that no one noticed.

But anyhow, they all grew up. I feel like their parent.
And just how much taller is Mako now?!

I KEPT YOU WAITING. SORRY!!
BA DUM
I'M READY NOW. LET'S GET GOING!
OH, THE PARTY IS TODAY THEN?
YUP. THAT'S RIGHT.
I WON'T BE BACK UNTIL TOMORROW. WILL YOU LET EVERYONE KNOW, NII-CHAN?
SURE.
DAZED

YOU KNOW, ITO-SAN...
SOMEHOW, YOU'VE...
YEAH...
...CHANGED.
YOU NEVER LOOKED LIKE...
HEY, GUYS!
DA
DUM
WHAT'S WRONG WITH YOU?
I'M STILL THE SAME!!
HER CRUDE TALK AND MANNERISMS HAVEN'T CHANGED, I GUESS.
YAH YAH
So cute
Did you do your hair yourself?
No, Yūto helped me this morning.
IT'S ALL RIGHT TO PARTY, BUT DON'T GET CARRIED AWAY, OKAY?
DON'T WORRY!

GOODBYE!
IT'S ONE MONTH AFTER GRADUATION.

WE'RE VISITING TSUGUMI-SEMPAI'S PLACE TODAY...
...FOR THE DRAMA CLUB'S GRADUATION PARTY.
TO BE FRANK, WE'RE ALL STARTING OUR NEW LIVES IN A FEW DAYS.
SO BEFORE WE DO, WE DECIDED TO HAVE A NIGHT OF FUN.
MAKOTO IS STILL BUSY WITH HIS JOB, AND HE'S SUPPOSED TO SHOW UP A LITTLE LATE TODAY.
WAIT. HE'S GRADUATED.
AND HE TOLD ME HE'D SHOW UP AS A GUY.
B-BMP B-BMP
I DON'T EVEN KNOW WHO'S COMING TO THE PARTY.
Would that be okay?
DO YOU REMEMBER TSUGUMI-SEMPAI'S...
...SECOND HOUSE WE STAYED AT FOR SUMMER TRAINING CAMP?
AH, YOU MEAN THE HOUSE LOADED WITH CONTRAPTIONS!
I HAVE A BAD FEELING...
Did you hear? Tsugumi-Sempai lives in a super plush house.
...
We'll get yummy treats!! Yay.
HANG ON, SECOND HOUSE AFTER ALL.
IT CAN'T BE THAT WAY IN A QUIET RESIDENTIAL NEIGHBORHOOD...
THAT'S SO TRUE!
PHEW
...WHERE PEOPLE LIVE LIKE EVERYONE ELSE.
Ah ha ha
SHE'S GOT FAMILY LIKE EVERYBODY ELSE.

SUMMARIZING FIVE YEARS

It's already been five years since I started drawing WJ. It sounds like a long time, but it passed so fast. It feels like five years vanished before I knew it.

Because it's the first time I worked on one title so long, it's natural that I became attached to the characters.

At this point, instead of me making them act, they start chatting on their own inside my brain. They even pulled a coup d'état many times!

I want the story to take this course.
No!
You can't settle the issue just like that.

DOOON
NOMURA
TEE HEE HEE. THANKS FOR COMING, FOLKS!!

I THOUGHT YOU'D ARRIVE BY NOW.
I WAS RIGHT ABOUT KEEPING AN EYE ON THE SECURITY VIDEO. ♡
BE GRATEFUL FOR THE DELUXE GUEST ROOMS I HAD PREPARED!
I'M SURE YOU'LL WORSHIP ME FOR THAT.
JUST USE THE INTERCOM!!
Mom, that lady...
Shh Don't look.
Poor thing.
WEL-COME.
KRRT
WEL-COME.
GRRT KRRT
WEL-COME.
I'VE GOT OTHER PLANS!
ME, TOO.
KLUTCH
!?
MAYBE I SHOULDN'T HAVE...
...COME TO THIS PARTY.
UGYAAH
AAHHH

?
DID I HEAR ITO-SAN SCREAM JUST NOW?
CHATTER CHATTER
OR WAS IT MY IMAGINATION?
KLIK
THE PARTY SHOULD'VE STARTED BY NOW.
April 3 6:30
SST
PLEASE GO AHEAD.
HEY, THANKS, MISTER!
LET ME JUST--
AH.
HUH?
DING DONG
THE TRAIN ARRIVING ON PLATFORM 2...
...IS AN EXPRESS HEADING FOR SHINJUKU.

CHATTER CHATTER
WOW.
I THOUGHT I WAS DUPED... ...BUT IT'S INCREDIBLY RICH!!
I'M JUST RELIEVED IT'S NORMAL INSIDE.
I didn't know what to think at first.
Soft, comfy sofa
CHAT CHAT
OH.
LONG TIME NO SEE, YOU GUYS.
HOW'RE YOU DOING?
MS. ITÔ!
YO, YOSHIRÔ.
OCHIAI!
Long time no see!
Gya ha ha ha. It's Been only a month, you idiot!
LOOKS LIKE MOST OF THE GRADUATES HAVE COME.
IS EVERYONE HERE NOW?
TOKI-SEMPAI SAID HE'D BE LATE, ITO-SAN.
WHAT?

TOKI-CHAN'S COMING?!
But it's a graduation party, isn't it?!
YUP.
SOME ALUMNI ARE INVITED, TOO, YOU KNOW?
AND THE PRETTIEST ONE IS ME!!
WHOA!!
ICHIJÔ-SEMPAI...
Appearing at the end
GOOD TO SEE YOU, GIRLS.
I HEARD ABOUT THE AUDITION.
TOO BAD. I WAS HOPING YOU'D JOIN OUR TROUPE.
OH.
Ha ha ha
DON'T MIND ME. MIYABI IS A GOOD ONE.
BUT... WHERE'S AMANO-SAN?
AH.
MIGHT BE LATE BECAUSE OF THE JOB.
YEAH?
HE'S REALLY LATE, THOUGH.
I THOUGHT HE SAID HE'D BE HERE BY 7 P.M.
CHATTER CHATTER

THERE'RE A GOOD NUMBER OF PEOPLE HERE.
I HOPE IT'S GONNA BE OKAY.
RU
SSSHHH

GET DOWN HERE! YOU BLOND JERK!!
LEMME FLATTEN YOU!
It's not that okay.
HOW COME HE'S LIKE THAT TO THE VERY END?
SINCE THE CULTURAL FESTIVAL, TOKI-SEMPAI STOPPED CHASING AFTER ITO-SAN...
...BUT I GUESS THIS IS A DIFFERENT ISSUE.
You punk! Face me!!
Hmph.
!

OKAY, LET'S START THE EVENT!
ALL GRADUATES MUST COME UP ON STAGE AND SHOUT YOUR ASPIRATIONS!
AND OF COURSE, ITO-KUN, YOU GO FIRST!
WHAAT?!
HUH?!

KLUCCH

?
WHAT'S THAT NOISE?
BEEP
BEEP
OH, AN INTRUDER.
SNAP

!
HOLD IT!
WSSH
WSSH
BEEP
BEEP

WHAT?
IT BEEPS WHEN SOMEONE ENTERS WITHOUT COMING THROUGH THE GATE.
TAP TAP
LET ME LAUNCH THE WELCOME OPERATION!
KLICK

WHAT DID YOU PRESS JUST NOW?!

WHAT'S WRONG WITH ALL OF YOU?
WE'RE TALKING ABOUT AN INTRUDER.

KA-RANGG
ELIMINATION IS THE ONLY WAY TO GO.

WHAT THE--??!

KLA
NGG
THE THING IS, THOUGH, I'M NOT SURE WHERE THE TRESPASSER WILL END UP.
NOT AGAIN!!
PLEASE THINK AHEAD JUST A LITTLE MORE!
FIP
FWIPP
HUH?
AH.

UGH.
KYAH
TOKI-SEMPAI!!
TH WACK
TUNK
?!
OH.
SO THIS IS WHERE IT'S CONNECTED TO.
MAKO!!
MAKOTO-SAN?!
ERUPT-iNG
WHAT?!
The hair!!
MURMUR
NO WAY! GOTTA BE KIDDING!
ISN'T HE A DIFFERENT PERSON WHO LOOKS LIKE HER?!
MURMUR
MURMUR
OH NO... HOW AM I GONNA EXPLAIN?
URM... IT'S ...
SST

!
THE MAN YOU SEE IN FRONT OF YOU...
...IS THE SAME PERSON AS MAKOTO AMANO...
...WHO WAS IN THE DRAMA CLUB WITH YOU.
WHAT?
BUT --
MURMUR
PLEASE LISTEN.
TODAY, I'VE COME IN MY NATURAL APPEARANCE...
...SO I CAN TELL YOU THE TRUTH.
LET ME RECOUNT WHAT ACTUALLY HAPPENED.

PLEASE LISTEN.
TAK

YOU OFTEN WATCH PARENTS ON TV...
HMPH.
...WHO'D SAY "NOT MY DAUGHTER!"
I GUESS THAT'S PRECISELY HOW I FEEL AT THE MOMENT.
A PILE OF DEAD BODIES.
...
There is no God!
HEH... SO YOU ARE A BOY, THEN....
HOW 'BOUT IT TONIGHT?
HUH?
THAT'S AN ODD ONE OVER THERE.
YOU'D BETTER WATCH OUT, ITO-KUN.
!!
HA HA HA
IT'S A JOKE! A JOKE!
No. You were serious!
TO TOP IT OFF, YOU TWO WERE ALREADY TOGETHER. HOW SHOCKING!
Totally unaffected
IT SURE IS!
NOOO! I DON'T WANNA HEAR IT!!
OMMP

GRR RR
HA! WHATEVER!
YOU'RE STILL THE SAME GUY WHO DUPED ME AND MADE FUN OF ME!!
GAK
!
OH NO! I FORGOT ABOUT HIM!
TOKI-SEMPAI, DON'T!!
FREEZE

DON'T I ALWAYS TELL YOU NOT TO RESORT TO VIOLENCE?!
ESPECIALLY NOT AT OUR GRADUATION PARTY!
SMAK SMAK SMAK
O--
OKAY. I'M SORRY.
HEY, DON'T CRY.
WHAT A SURPRISE...
A LION WHO'S SCARED OF A POMERANIAN, HUH?

Hey, Guys! Get up!
Let's continue the party!
Yeees.
SLUMP
I HAD NO IDEA AT ALL.
I sure didn't
BUT...
I'M SERIOUSLY STUNNED.
THEY SURE WERE GOOD FRIENDS.
BUT...

MISAKI-CHAN, IT'S YOUR TURN.
WHAT'S YOUR ASPIRATION?!
YES.
IT'S NO WONDER ITO-SAN GOT PRETTIER.
TMP TMP
MISAKI AND NOBUKO ARE BOTH GOING TO THE SAME JUNIOR COLLEGE, RIGHT?
YOU WON'T BE ABLE TO SEE HER AS OFTEN, HUH?
SMIRK
Hmph
I DON'T WANNA GO TO COLLEGE AND STUDY MORE.
Can't go anyway
IT'S OKAY. I'M GONNA WORK AND SAVE SOME MONEY.
EVEN IF I GET TO SEE HER LESS...
...IT ONLY MEANS I CAN ASK HER TO MARRY ME SOONER, RIGHT?
My aspiration is to be a bride.♥
Ah ha ha Good one!

HMMM. DIDN'T KNOW YOU HAD THAT IN MIND.
I'M A MAN AFTER ALL.
HEY, MAKOTO-SAN, IS IT OKAY TO TURN YOUR STORY INTO A NOVEL?
WHAT?
BUT I HEAR YOU GOT A JOB THROUGH YOUR FAMILY CONNECTIONS.
An auto parts manufacturing company, right?
THAT'S NOT THE POINT, OKAY!
GYA HA HA
Not so cool
I MEAN, CAN I USE IT AS A MODEL?!
BA —DUMM
TEE HEE HEE HEE. I'M NOT GONNA BE BEATEN BY YOU, MAKOTO AMANO!
IT NO LONGER MATTERS IF YOU'RE A MAN OR A WOMAN!
EITHER WAY, I'M THE ONE WHO'LL BE WITH ITO-KUN!!

SHE'S THE ONLY ONE WHO DOESN'T CHANGE NO MATTER HOW MANY YEARS PASS.
Attacking for an unknown reason
Stop right there!
I HEAR TSUGUMI-SEMPAI WANTS TO BE AN INTERIOR DECORATOR.
BUT SHE'S BETTER SUITED AS AN INVENTOR.
THERE'S A PROBLEM TO THAT, TOO.
Seriousy
WE'RE ALL TAKING STEPS TOWARD OUR DREAMS.
WHEN WE'RE MUCH OLDER...

I WONDER HOW...
...WE'LL LOOK BACK ON OUR HIGH SCHOOL DAYS.

THEY'RE BEING...

...TOO WILD OVER THERE.

GYA HA HA HA

MS. ITÔ, WE WANT SOME BOOZE, TOO!

CHATTER CHATTER

YOU'RE TOO YOUNG!

WHERE'S THE BATHROOM?

THERE'S ONE AT THE END OF THE HALLWAY.

CRMBL

?

Wanna get away together?

MAKOTO.
HUH?
WHAT'S WRONG, MISAKI?
WELL...
I DON'T SEE...
...THOSE TWO ANY-WHERE...

IT FEELS GREAT...
...TO BE ABLE TO WALK WITH YOU LIKE THIS!
YUP. DON'T NEED TO WORRY ABOUT BEING SEEN ANYMORE.
LET'S WALK AROUND IN BROAD DAYLIGHT NEXT TIME.
SURE. IT'S TOO BAD IT'S NIGHTTIME.
ASBee
CHATTER
CHATTER
SO...
WHERE DO YOU WANNA GO?
I'LL GO ANYPLACE YOU WANT, ITO-SAN.
AT THIS HOUR, I GUESS AN AMUSEMENT PARK WOULDN'T DO.
HA HA HA.
Hmph.
...
ALL RIGHT. GOTTA GO THERE THEN!
HM?

THE SCHOOL!

MAYBE BECAUSE I WAS HERE EVERY DAY...
I MISS THE PLACE ALREADY. BUT IT'S BEEN ONLY A MONTH SINCE GRADUATION.
WE HAVE LOTS OF MEMORIES HERE.

IT'S WHERE I MET YOU, MAKO.

DO YOU WANT TO...

...LOOK IN THE GYM?

RATTLE
HEY.
I THINK I WAS RIGHT HERE WHEN WE FIRST MET.
AND YOU, ITO-SAN, STOOD RIGHT AROUND WHERE YOU ARE.
YEAH, YOU REMEMBER THAT?

"WHERE IS THE TEACHER FOR THE DRAMA CLUB?"
LOOKING BACK, WE'VE BOTH CHANGED A LOT, DON'T YOU THINK?

YEAH, WE'RE A TOTALLY REVERSED COUPLE.
ITO-SAN, YOU'VE BECOME SO FEMININE...
You're so cute. ♥
YOU'VE CHANGED, TOO.
WELL...IT'S LIKE WE WENT BACK TO OUR NATURAL FORMS AFTER GRADUATION... SORT OF...

OUR LOOKS MIGHT HAVE CHANGED...
...BUT MY PASSION FOR ACTING...
...AND MY AFFECTION FOR YOU, ITO-SAN, WILL NEVER CHANGE.

I PROMISE.
A LOT HAPPENED IN THIS GYM.
IT'S WHERE WE STARTED.

UNDOUBTEDLY, HE'S THE ONE...
...WHO CHANGED ME FROM WHO I WAS.
EACH MEMORY WE SHARE TOGETHER...
...IS WHAT REALLY STARTED MY LIFE.
I GUESS... WE WON'T BE VISITING HERE AGAIN FOR A WHILE.
DOES IT MAKE YOU FEEL SAD?
NOPE. NOT REALLY.
WOW, SO CERTAIN.
'CAUSE I HAVE THE THEATER.
AND YOU, MAKOTO, WITH ME.

WE'VE GOT LOTS OF DREAMS WE'RE GONNA ACHIEVE.
AND WE'VE GOT NO TIME TO STAND STILL!

THAT AUTUMN, MAKOTO DEFINITELY WAS THERE.
AND I DEFINITELY WAS HERE.
I STILL HAVE MANY VIVID MEMORIES.

KEEPING THE IRREPLACEABLE DAYS IN OUR HEARTS...

...WE WILL WALK ON THE PATH OF LIGHT.
W JULIET 14 ⑭ / THE END

SUPER FINAL EVENT W JULIET CHARACTER CONTEST RESULTS ANNOUNCEMENT!!

NOW, HERE ARE THE CHARACTERS WHO DID NOT MAKE IT TO THE TOP FIVE. THERE ARE CHARACTERS FROM WAY BACK WHEN, TOO.

7 YOSHIRÔ OZAKI

EMURA: I ENJOYED DRAWING HIS FRIENDSHIP WITH ITO! HE WAS MY IDEA OF AN "ORDINARY" PERSON.

6 AKANE NARITA

EMURA: THE ONE AND ONLY NORMAL FEMALE OF THE NARITA FAMILY. (LAUGH) SHE WORKED HARD ON BEHALF OF ITO AND MAKOTO!!

10 NOBUKO KATAOKA

EMURA: SHE WAS A CHARACTER SO CUTE AND EASY TO DRAW.♥ HER UNIQUE HAIRSTYLE WAS MY FAVORITE.

9 CHRIS-TINA

EMURA: DESPITE HER LATE APPEARANCE, HER POPULARITY IS IMPRESSIVE. SHE WAS A FUN CHARACTER.

8 MISAO TOKI

EMURA: HE'S SOMEONE WHO SPLIT THE READERS VIOLENTLY IN THEIR OPINIONS. AS THE AUTHOR, I'M RELIEVED TO FIND HIM WINNING EIGHTH PLACE.

11: TSUBAKI NARITA; SATSUKI MIURA
13: MISAKI ICHIKAWA
14: TAKAYO IIZUKA
15: YUTAKA SAKAMOTO
16: SAKURA SUGIYAMA
17: GORÔ MIURA; MASUMI NARITA
19: TSUGUMI NOMURA; JÔTARO KAI
21: RISA NARITA; SHINOBU
23: MITSUKO MIURA; TOMOE MIURA
25: KÔHEI TAKADA; SATOSHI
27: RIE TSUNODA

THE CHARACTER CONTEST WAS FULL OF SURPRISES, WITH MYSELF MAKING THE RANK! ♥

28: IKKEI
29: MS. EMURA; SWAN; MERMAID
32: MS. ITÔ; ATSUSHI ICHIJÔ; TAIKI SUGIYAMA
35: MEGUMI SEMPAI; THREE ROBBERS
37: TAKASHI IIZUKA; DIRECTOR IGARASHI; SAYOKO

← SEE PAGE 162 FOR BEST COUPLE AWARDS!

W Juliet

—SUMMER DAYS—

SUPER FINAL EVENT

W JULIET BEST COUPLE AWARDS RESULTS ANNOUNCEMENT!!

FOR THE BEST COUPLE AWARDS, WE ASKED THE READERS TO VOTE ALONG WITH THE CHARACTER CONTEST. ITO AND MAKOTO ARE EXCLUDED FROM THE RACE. WHICH COUPLE TURNED OUT TO BE THE BEST?

YÛTO MIURA & AKANE NARITA

EMURA: I HAD A FEELING THIS WOULD BE THE CASE. THEY'RE THE ONE AND ONLY QUIET COUPLE IN *WJ*. (LAUGH) I WISH THEM HAPPINESS. ♥

2

YOSHIRÔ OZAKI & MISAKI ICHIKAWA

EMURA: I'M GLAD THEY MADE SECOND PLACE. I HAD FUN DRAWING YOSHIRÔ TIED TO MISAKI'S APRON STRINGS.

3

RYÛYA MIURA & CHRISTINA

EMURA: IN A SENSE, THEY WERE THE MOST OUTRAGEOUS COUPLE... IT WAS EXHILARATING TO HAVE THEM AS COMIC RELIEF. ♪

4: MISAO TOKI & NOBUKO KATAOKA
5: YOSHIRÔ OZAKI & ITO MIURA
6: RYÛYA MIURA & YÛTO MIURA
7: TATSUYOSHI MIURA & RIE TSUNODA
8: GORÔ MIURA & SATSUKI MIURA
9: MISAO TOKI & TSUGUMI NOMURA
10: RYÛYA MIURA & ITO MIURA

OVERALL COMMENT FROM MS. EMURA

THE RESULTS WERE WAY BEYOND WHAT I ANTICIPATED AND QUITE ENJOYABLE. "WOW, IS THAT WHAT THEY THINK?!" I EXCLAIMED AS I REACKNOWLEDGED THE CHARACTERS' DIFFERENT POPULARITY LEVELS. (LAUGH) THANKS AGAIN FOR SENDING MANY VOTES. I WAS VERY HAPPY THAT WE WERE ABLE TO HAVE THE CHARACTER CONTEST AT THE END.

TATSU-YOSHI-KUN!
REE REE REEE
HUH?
TUNK
LOOK AT THIS!
IS IT TRUE THAT YOUR SISTER IS IN THIS PLAY?!
YEAH. A SMALL ROLE, THOUGH.
IT'S HER FIRST PLAY AFTER A WHOLE YEAR.
YOU SERIOUS?! IT'S AWESOME!
LIKE I SAID, IT'S JUST A SMALL ROLE.
BUT THAT'S INCREDIBLE! MIYABI IS A WELL-KNOWN TROUPE, ISN'T IT?
THEATER SCHEDULE
BALLET GROUP
TROUPE MIYABI

—Behind the Scenes Story ⑥—

I thought I could draw a lot in 40 pages, but it turned out I hardly had enough space and subcharacters' scenes had to be cut right and left. (Sob) I'm sorry if you expected a lot!

Regarding their marriage, I felt that was just about right, and I didn't draw the wedding scene on purpose. Oh well, if I had another 20 pages maybe they might've had one.

Apparently, they think "living together" is more important than having a wedding ceremony.

COME TO THINK OF IT, I'VE NEVER MET TATSUYOSHI-KUN'S SISTER.
WHAT'S SHE LIKE?
Is she pretty?
I HEAR SHE RESEMBLES TATSUYOSHI.
Whaat?
Ah ha ha
?
Hmph
THAT'S WHEN SHE WAS STILL A STUDENT.
SHE CHANGED QUITE A BIT IN A YEAR.
YAAHHHH
KLAP
KLAP
YAAHHH
KLAP
KLAP
KLAP
NICE WORK, EVERYONE!
HEY! WE GOT FLOWERS!

Now the last one. Readers often ask me which character is my favorite. I guess it's too much to say I like them all. (Laugh) If I have to choose one, I say it's Ryûya. I love both looking at and drawing a hot-blooded Nii-chan like him. ♪
I bet I'll include that type of character again in my next title.

Well, there's hardly any space left. Please make a note of the tiny information I included at the end of the volume.

Thanks again for your longtime support!

2003.2.9
Emura

OH, THANKS, MIURA-SAN. ♡
CHATTER
NICE WORK!
TONS OF PEOPLE CAME AGAIN.
I HEAR WE'RE SOLD OUT EVERY DAY.
Good job.
REALLY?
BUT YOU KNOW...
CHATTER
THERE'S NO ONE WHO LOOKS AS GOOD AS ITO-SAN IN GUYS' CLOTHES. ♥
AS SOON AS SHE STARTS ACTING, SHE BECOMES EVEN MORE MANLY.
THE AUDIENCE WAS CHECKING HER OUT.
HUH?
IS IT TRUE YOU USED TO HAVE YOUR HAIR SHORT WHEN YOU WERE A STUDENT?
AND WORE A BOY'S SCHOOL UNIFORM?
WOW, I WANNA SEE HER IN THAT!
CHATTER
YOU'RE NOT DOING THAT ANYMORE?
CHATTER
ER... THAT...?
Only when acting now...
NOK NOK

KACHAK
EXCUSE ME.
THE DIRECTOR IS ABOUT TO START THE MEETING.
WILL YOU ALL COME TO THE CONFERENCE ROOM?
MAKO!
AND HIM... WHY IS IT THAT HE LOOKS SO GREAT IN WOMEN'S CLOTHES...?
WHEN HE'S USUALLY A NORMAL GUY...
He's beautiful no matter when I look at him!
Haaa. He's like candy to the eyes.
That's what's great about him!
HEY, IS IT TRUE THEY'RE DATING?
APPARENTLY SINCE THEIR HIGH SCHOOL DAYS.
WOW. SINCE HIGH SCHOOL...
SINCE HIGH SCHOOL?
I HEAR MIURA-SAN USED TO BE TALLER BACK THEN.

Dressed as a man → and taller.
←BOY
...
I WONDER WHICH ONE CONFESSED THEIR LOVE FIRST...
Dunno...
Wanna know...
CHATTER
CHATTER
MEMBERS OF THE THEATER HAVE NO IDEA ABOUT MAKOTO'S PAST.
OVER A YEAR HAS PASSED SINCE WE GRADUATED FROM HIGH SCHOOL.
AND THIS SUMMER, WE MADE OUR MEMORABLE DEBUT.
I AM GLAD I COULD TAKE...
...THE FIRST STEP OF MY ACTING CAREER TOGETHER WITH MAKOTO.
BUT... THINKING HIGHLY OF OUR EXPERIENCE AS STUDENTS (?)...
...DIRECTOR KAI MARKED US...
Only one in the theater troupe who knows.
Heh Aren't they great characters
What ?!
Script
...AND GOT US TO PLAY A DRAMA WITH A MAN AND A WOMAN SWAPPED.
BUT IT'S ONLY WHEN WE'RE ACTING.
See you tomorrow!
Bye.

KLAP
WE PRETTY MUCH LOOK LIKE THIS NOW.
GOOD JOB, MAKO!
YOU, TOO, ITO-SAN.
IT'LL BE ALL OVER IN A WEEK, HUH?
A MONTH PASSES SO FAST.
CHATTER
CHATTER
HEY, ITO-SAN, ABOUT THE RENTAL
I FOUND A GOOD ONE.
YOU SERIOUS?
I'M THINKING OF GOING OVER THERE TODAY. HOW ABOUT IT?
APARTMENT RENTAL
RUSTLE
WOW, I WANNA GO!
AH.
IF SEATING MAP
TATSU-YOSHI!
WHAT... ARE YOU DOING HERE?!
? ?
OH... WE SORT OF STOPPED BY...
...ON THE WAY BACK FROM SCHOOL.
WHAT? YOUR SISTER?
SHE'S PRETTY. ♡

HOW DO YOU DO?! I'M RIE TSUNODA.
AND I'M KOEDA KAWAGUCHI.
WHAT? YOU'VE GOT TWO GIRLFRIENDS?
NO WAY!
WHAT ABOUT YOU, NEE-CHAN? WHAT'S THAT THING?
ARE YOU GONNA TRY LIVING ALONE OR WHAT?
WHAT?
FLUP
APARTMENT RENTAL
2DK
OH... ER... WELL...
...
IT'S...
...
KLU
DD
GONNA LIVE TOGETHER?!

KEEP YOUR VOICE DOWN, YOU MORON!
WHAT IF THERE'S SOMEONE WE KNOW HERE!!
NUR
NUR
ITO-SAN, CALM DOWN.
AND SIT DOWN.
CHATTER
CHATTER
Attracting BIG attention
BUT... IT SHOCKED ME. IT'S A NORMAL REACTION!
D— DO YOU EVEN HAVE THE MONEY?!
Practical
YEAH... WE'LL MANAGE SOMEHOW...
...WITH OUR PART-TIME JOBS AND SAVINGS!
I ASKED HER...
...IF SHE'D WANT TO LIVE WITH ME SOMEWHERE NEAR THE TROUPE.
...
A STUDIO WOULD BE TOO SMALL, SO WE NEED A TWO-BEDROOM...
...THAT PERMITS PETS, AND THAT'S CLOSE TO THE BEACH.
Heh heh
MY DREAM IS TO OWN A DOG. ♪
WE HAD TO SEARCH A LOT, BUT IT LOOKS LIKE WE FOUND A GOOD PLACE.
TUNK
WE'RE ABOUT TO GO OVER THERE TODAY.
HUH?!
HANG ON...
IS IT OKAY TO DECIDE JUST LIKE THAT?
DAD DOESN'T KNOW ABOUT IT, RIGHT?!
WE'RE JUST GONNA GO LOOK AT IT.
AND I'LL TALK TO THE FAMILY PROPERLY.

PRO-PERLY?
WHEN?
NEXT WEEK.
THE LAST DAY OF THE RUN.
I INVITED MY PARENTS, TOO.
WE'RE THINKING OF TALKING ABOUT MANY THINGS.
HEY, NEE-CHAN!
IT'S STILL A SECRET, SO DON'T TELL ANYONE, OKAY?
IT'S GONNA BE FINE. I LEARNED HOW TO COOK OVER THE PAST YEAR. SO DON'T WORRY!
...
HMPH. TATSUYOSHI, YOU'RE PRETTY ATTACHED TO YOUR SISTER, HUH?
WHAT A SUR-PRISE.
SLURP
...
DAMMIT. LIVING TOGETHER?!
SHE SAID WHATEVER SHE WANTED TO SAY.
BUT SOMEHOW, I'M REALLY MAD!!
I BET YOU DON'T WANT HER TO LEAVE WITH THAT GUY.
IT'S NOT LIKE THAT!

BE HONEST.
...
IT'S GOTTEN REALLY LATE.
OH WELL, WE FOUND A NICE APARTMENT.
A TWO-BEDROOM PLACE, SUNNY, AND PETS ARE OKAY.
EXCITED
NOT CLOSE TO THE BEACH, BUT STILL IT'S GREAT.
Cheap, too!
BUT WE'LL HAVE TO WAIT UNTIL AFTER THE LAST RUN BEFORE WE SIGN THE CONTRACT.
WON'T SOMEONE ELSE SNATCH IT AWAY?
WE PUT DOWN A DEPOSIT, SO IT SHOULD BE OKAY.
I'm home!
DAD? WHAT'RE YOU DOING OUT HERE?
GOOD EVENING.
I WALKED ITO-SAN HOME.
SHK

GAK! MAKOTO-SAN?!
WHAT?
IT'S BAD, ITO. GET AWAY FAST!
DAD IS TOO DANGEROUS RIGHT NOW!
KIDS! SNEAKING BEHIND YOUR PARENTS' BACKS!!
WHOOSH
The neighbor's wall
WHOA!!
IS IT TRUE YOU'RE GONNA LIVE WITH MAKOTO-SAN?!
KRAM
?!
BEFORE YOU FIND A PLACE, YOU'VE GOTTA TALK TO DAD FIRST!!
TATSUYOSHI TOLD US ALL ABOUT IT!
You idiot!
YAY, IT SERVES YOU RIGHT.

YOU JERK... I TOLD YOU IT'S A SECRET!!
I DIDN'T PROMISE ANYTHING!
Heh heh
YOU SHOULD GET IN A LITTLE TROUBLE OVER THIS!
LIEUTEN-ANT, BRAKE!!
COME DOWN HERE, PUNK!
LET'S TALK IT OVER.
DON'T SAY IT LIKE A HAUGHTY COCK FROM UP THERE!
BUT YOU'LL KILL HIM IF HE COMES DOWN...

DAD, WE WERE GONNA TALK TO YOU ABOUT IT PROPERLY.
BESIDES, WE INVITED MAKO'S DAD TO THE LAST RUN, TOO.
WHAT?
I APOLOGIZE FOR MOVING AHEAD, BUT WE ARE VERY SERIOUS ABOUT THIS!

...
I SEE... THAT'S WHY YOU ASKED ME TO COME ON THE LAST DAY.
WELL... I WANT YOU TO SEE ME ACT, TOO.
AWKWARD
I'M NOT COMING.
A KID.
A BIG KID...
Huh ?!
PLEASE DON'T SAY THAT, SIR.
TUMP
GRRR
DON'T TELL ME WHAT TO DO!!

WHAT PARENT FEELS GOOD WHEN KIDS SET THINGS UP BEHIND THEIR BACKS LIKE THAT?!

STMP STMP

DAD!

Not again

I SAID I'M NOT COMING. THAT'S FINAL!!

THAT WASN'T ...

...THE BEST APPROACH, TATSUYOSHI.

Hmph

IT WASN'T MY FAULT.

K-RAK

HUH?
I BET YOU BROUGHT IT UP IN THE MOST UPSETTING WAY!
HEY.
I MEAN, IT'S YOU WHO TOLD HIM.
Ouch
STMP STMP
KEEPING IT A SECRET WAS WRONG!!
STMP
SHE'S IN HER MENAC-ING MODE...
WSSH
AH, GIVE IT BACK!
A RENTAL AGREEMENT?
SNEER

HA! IF YOU WANT IT BACK, COME GET IT!
TRUM TRUM TRUM
ITO-SAN!
SHE'S ABOUT TO LEAVE THE NEST, HUH?
TOO BAD DAD ISN'T WEANED FROM HER YET.
It's a prob-lem
WOOSH
YOU BRAT!!
HUH?
I DON'T REMEMBER TATSUYOSHI BEING THIS FAST.
RSSSH
Huff
Huff
ENRAGED
HE GOT AWAY!
ITO-SAN!
ENRAGED

HIS BODY GREW BIGGER, BUT HOW COME HIS BRAIN HASN'T CHANGED AT ALL!!
Dammit!
You haven't changed much either.
AS SOON AS I FIND HIM, I'M GONNA SMASH HIM!
WHY IS HE DOING THIS?!
...
Rental Agreement
Landlord and tenant agree as follows:
Address:
Phone:
WHAT WAS I THINKING?
WHAT DO I DO WITH THIS?
...
...
RASH

KLUTCH
WHOA.
EXCUSE ME, HOW MUCH IS THIS?
YOU'RE A GRADE SCHOOL STUDENT, AREN'T YOU?
WHAT'RE YOU DOING OUT THIS LATE? YOUR PARENTS WILL BE WORRIED.
IT'S 120 YEN.*
WH--!
SHUT UP!
*A little over $1.00
BESIDES, IT'S 10 YEARS TOO SOON TO STEAL.
I MEAN, EVEN AFTER 10 YEARS, JUST DON'T DO IT.
IT'S NONE OF YOUR BUSINESS!
I'M GONNA BE A GANGSTER!
IS HE A RUNAWAY?
YOU'VE ALREADY FAILED ONCE TO START WITH...
WH-- WHO CARES!
JUST LEAVE ME ALONE!
HEY, WHAT'S YOUR ADD-RESS?
I'LL TAKE YOU HOME.
IGNORING HIM.
...

KIDS NOWADAYS ARE NOT SO CUTE.
HOP
ACK
GRAB
WATCH OUT!
WHAT'RE YOU DOING, YOU IDIOT!!
TUNK
STMP
STMP
HEY!
HOLD IT RIGHT THERE!
HONNK
THIS BRAT!
WHAT THE HECK?

WHAT DOES HE WANT?!
RN NCH
WORN OUT
HUFF HUFF
RAILROAD CROSSING NOW?
YOU SAY YOU'RE GONNA BE A GANGSTER, BUT YOU'RE TRYING TO KILL YOURSELF INSTEAD.
Hey, move the leg
TUG
WHAT MADE YOU RUN AWAY FROM HOME?
TUG
Yeah, let's talk about it.
ONEE-CHAN...
...IS GETTING MARRIED.
!
AND ...
...OUR DOG HAD PUPPIES.
YOUR STORY IS JUMPING ALL OVER THE MAP...
SHE'S TAKING A PUPPY WITH HER...
...BUT SHE'S LEAVING ME BEHIND...
...BUT I WAS THERE BEFORE THE PUPPY.
THAT'S WHY...

...SHE SHOULD BE UPSET A LITTLE...
...WITH ME DOING BAD THINGS AND GETTING HURT.
IT'LL SERVE HER RIGHT.
"YOU SHOULD GET IN A LITTLE TROUBLE OVER THIS!"
...
THAT'S WHY IT'S OKAY TO GET HURT.
ONII-CHAN, YOU DON'T HAVE TO HELP ME ANYMORE.
HUH? WHAT'RE YOU TALKING ABOUT?
Man.
IF THE TRAIN COMES, YOU'RE DEAD MEAT--
TANG
TANG
TANG

TANG
TANG
TANG
TANG
TANG

GEEZ.
WHERE THE HECK DID HE GO?!
He makes me so mad!
STMP
STMP
HE WASN'T AT THE ARCADE.

I FELT THIS STRANGE VIBE.
HE DOESN'T WANT ME, DOES HE?
HE FINDS IT ENTERTAINING TO SEE ME IN TROUBLE. THAT'S ALL.
TANG
TANG
TANG
TANG

?!
WHAT'S THAT?
YEAH.
A KID'S VOICE?
TANG
TANG
TANG

WHY DID YOU STICK YOUR FOOT INTO THIS?!
BECAUSE!!
TUGG
HOW DID YOU DO IT?! COME ON!!
WHOOO
WAHHH
ONEE-CHAN!
IF YOU WERE GONNA CRY, YOU SHOULD'VE NEVER DONE IT!
TATSUYOSHI?!
!!
ITO-SAN, STAY RIGHT THERE.
MAKO!
TANG
TANG
TANG
TANG
TANG
YEAH.
I'M JUST LIKE YOU.
TANG
TANG
TANG

I'M A KID WHO'S NOT READY.
BUT I DON'T KNOW WHAT TO DO.
I'M A FOOL. THIS IS JUST WHAT I END UP DOING.
REGULAR
TATSU--
TATSUYOSHI!!

GRUM
GRUM
GRUM
GRUM
GRUM
GRUM

WAH
WAHHH
OUCH.
WAAHHHH
HIS SHOE IS A WRECK, THOUGH.
A CLOSE CALL...
MAKOTO -SA--
Gak
SLAMM

KRAM
BAM
OUCH.
OU-OUCH.
KRAK
STOP IT, NEE-CHAN...
AHHH
WA
"BE HONEST."
AHHH
W
I'M SORRY, NEE-CHAN.

I'M SORRY...
AFTER THAT, TATSUYOSHI SAID NOTHING.
AND MY FAMILY CALMED DOWN.
DAD STILL INSISTS HE WON'T COME TO THE LAST RUN.
AND WE...
WHAT?
YOU CANCELED THE CONTRACT?

WHY? I THOUGHT YOU GUYS WERE SERIOUS ABOUT IT.
?!
WE ARE. OUR WISH HASN'T CHANGED.
WE'RE BASICALLY DELAYING IT.
I JUST HAVE THIS FEELING...
...THAT IT MIGHT BE BETTER IF I STAYED HERE A LITTLE LONGER.
...
KACHAK
WHAT'S UP, TATSUYOSHI? YOU'RE STILL AWAKE.
...
URM, YÛTO...
YEAH?

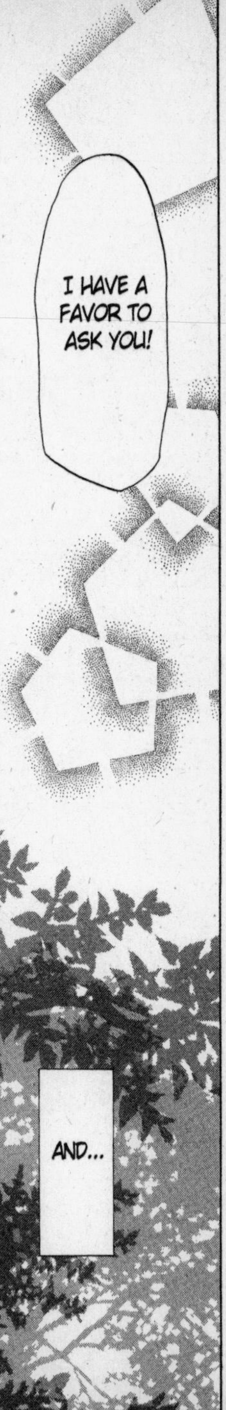
I HAVE A FAVOR TO ASK YOU!
AND...

...THE LAST DAY OF THE RUN HAS ARRIVED.
CHATTER
CHATTER
CHATTER
GLOOM...
WHAT'S WRONG WITH MIURA-SAN?
SHE SEEMS DOWN.
MURMUR
MURMUR
USUALLY, SHE'S FULL OF SPUNK...
It's unusual

AT THE END... I COULDN'T PERSUADE DAD.
SO I WONDER HOW IT'LL WORK OUT TODAY.
ITO-SAN.
DON'T WORRY, MAKO.
I'LL PULL MYSELF TOGETHER BY THE TIME IT STARTS.

I'LL GREET MAKO'S FATHER.
AS FOR MY DAD ...
WE'LL APPROACH HIM LATER--
YUP.
I SHOULD FOCUS ON THE PLAY.
LET ME THINK MORE AFTER IT'S OVER.

DAD?!
WHAT?!
HOW COME?
WHEN HE WAS SO INSISTENT!
WHY IS HE HERE?!
BA-DUM

GRR
I HEAR YOU'VE TAKEN GOOD CARE OF MY STUPID SON...
...
OH, NOT AT ALL ...
DID YOU HEAR ABOUT THEIR RELATION-SHIP?
GRR GRR GRR
...
YES, OVER THE PHONE SOME TIME AGO.
Hmmm
LET ME HEAR WHAT YOU HAVE TO SAY ABOUT IT...

N--NII-CHAN, CAN YOU DO SOMETHING ABOUT THIS ATMO-SPHERE?
BESIDES, HOW DID YOU GET DAD TO COME?!
WELL, IT WAS SOME... PROCESS.
HONEY, STOP GLARING LIKE THAT.
OTHERWISE, OUR CONVER-SATION WON'T MOVE FORWARD.
CHNK

HM... IT'S...
THIS RESTAU-RANT'S FLAN CARAMEL.
THE PLACE IS KNOWN FOR IT.
HM. IT'S PRETTY GOOD.

CUSTARD WORKS BEST FOR FLAN.
HA HA HA
OH, MIURA-SAN, YOU LIKE THEM, TOO?
L--LOOK, THEY'RE SOMEHOW GETTING ALONG.
FLAN'S INCRED-IBLE.
CHNK
ITO.
WHETHER IT'S NOW OR A YEAR FROM NOW,
IF YOU WANT TO LIVE TOGETHER...
...DO IT RIGHT.
DO IT RIGHT ?
PLUM ROOM

I'M TALKING ABOUT MARRIAGE.
AS A PARENT, I CAN'T LET YOU MOVE OUT...
...IF YOU HAVE NO PLANS TO MARRY.
It's not accept-able.
KA-TUNK
HANG ON, DAD. YOU WERE AGAINST--
I'M NOT AGAINST IT. I JUST DON'T LIKE IT WHEN IT'S NOT DONE OPENLY.
...
IT'S OKAY THEN?

THE DISCUSSION BETWEEN OUR TWO FAMILIES...
...CAME TO AN UNEXPECTED CLOSE.

WHETHER MAKO'S DAD KNEW OR DIDN'T KNOW...
...HE LEFT MY PAST RELATIONSHIP WITH MAKO UNQUESTIONED.

HE'S A DIFFICULT PERSON AS HE'S ALWAYS BEEN, AND I COULDN'T CHAT MUCH WITH HIM.

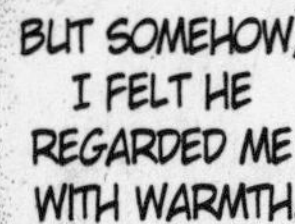
BUT SOMEHOW, I FELT HE REGARDED ME WITH WARMTH.

WOW, WHEN THINGS GET SETTLED, IT SURE HAPPENS ALL AT ONCE!

OH... BUT THE APARTMENT...
We missed out on that one.
WE'LL HAVE TO LOOK AGAIN.
CHATTER
CHATTER
Hey.
It's me.
HA HA HA. SOUNDS LIKE YOU'RE READY TO ROLL!
Dad went home alone.
ER... RYÛYA-SAN, WHERE'RE WE GOING FROM HERE?
HM?
WHERE DO YOU THINK?
SHABBY
...
WHAT'S THIS PLACE...?
HEY, YOU'RE HERE.
KACHAK
YÛTO'S HERE?! AND TATSUYOSHI, TOO!
What're you doing?
JUST GET INSIDE!
PUSH PUSH
HEY! WHAT?!
FWASSH

!
DESPITE HOW IT LOOKS OUTSIDE ...
IT'S PRETTY NICE IN HERE.
YEAH.
WE FIXED IT UP, YOU KNOW.
HUH?
Ito
FIFTEEN MINUTES FROM THE TRAIN STATION.
TWENTY MINUTES TO THE BEACH. TEN MINUTES TO THE TROUPE.
PETS OKAY. SUNNY AND BRIGHT. IT'S SHABBY, BUT IT'S A HOUSE WITH A YARD.
FOR RENT
15 MIN. WALK FROM Y STATION.
AND BRIGHT! PETS OKAY.
THEY SAID THEY'D RENT IT FOR CHEAP IF WE FIXED IT UP OURSELVES.
PRETTY NICE, ISN'T IT?
It used to be a piano school.

HUH?!
A house?!
NO ONE TOLD ME ABOUT THIS...!
When did you find it?
OF COURSE, IT WAS A SECRET.
IT WAS TATSUYOSHI WHO SUGGESTED THAT...
...WE FIND A PLACE THAT MEETS YOUR REQUIREMENTS.
INCIDENTALLY, HE'S THE ONE WHO PERSUADED DAD.
DAD WAS SHOCKED TO BE LECTURED BY THE LIKES OF HIM.
...
ER... I WAS SORRY ABOUT THE OTHER DAY.
I FELT NERVOUS ABOUT LOSING A FAMILY MEMBER.
I GUESS THAT'S WHY I DID WHAT I DID.
BUT I'M OKAY NOW.
I'M HAPPY FOR YOU BOTH, NEE-CHAN AND MAKOTO-SAN.
I WISH YOU THE VERY BEST.

NEE-CHAN IS A SHREW...
...BUT PLEASE LOOK AFTER HER, MAKOTO-SAN!
The shrew part was unnecessary!
But you are!
I HAVE MAKOTO ...
...AND MY FAMILY.
I AM SUPER HAPPY TODAY.
REMEMBER THAT BOY FROM THE OTHER DAY? THEY SAID THEY'D GIVE YOU...
...ONE OF THEIR PUPPIES.
YOU SERIOUS ?
YUP.
I'M SO GLAD I HAVE ALL OF THEM.
WE WILL...

...HAVE A HAPPY LIFE TOGETHER NO MATTER WHAT.
JULY 23
OH, WHERE'S ITO?
AT CITY HALL WITH MAKOTO-SAN.
THEY'RE STOPPING BY THEIR PLACE ON THE WAY BACK.
Yeah, sure
IT'LL BE A WHILE BEFORE THEY CAN MOVE IN.
THEY'RE GETTING MARRIED ON ITO'S BIRTHDAY.
AND WHY NOT?
IT'S THEIR SPECIAL DAY AFTER ALL.
IT SURE IS.
SPARKLE
SPARKLE
SPARKLE
SPARKLE
GOOD.

WE PRETTY MUCH DECIDED WHERE THINGS WILL GO.
BUT ISN'T THIS BED TOO BIG?
IT'S BETTER THAN SMALL.
IT'S ALL RIGHT SINCE WE'LL BE SLEEPING ON IT TOGETHER. ♪

Y--YEAH, RIGHT.
BLUSSH
WE GOT OUR PAPERWORK DONE, BUT I GUESS...
...YOU DON'T REALLY FEEL LIKE WE'RE MARRIED YET.
You're so cute
Yup

HOW ABOUT STAYING HERE FOR THE NIGHT?
WHAT?
IF YOU DON'T WANT TO, IT'S OKAY.
I'LL DO WHATEVER YOU WANT, ITO-SAN.

WHAT DO YOU THINK?

UM.
UM.
...

I WOULDN'T MIND IT...

LET'S LIVE TOGETHER WITH A DOG...
...IN A SMALL HOUSE WHERE WE CAN SEE THE OCEAN...
...AND LEAD A HAPPY LIFE FOREVER AND EVER.

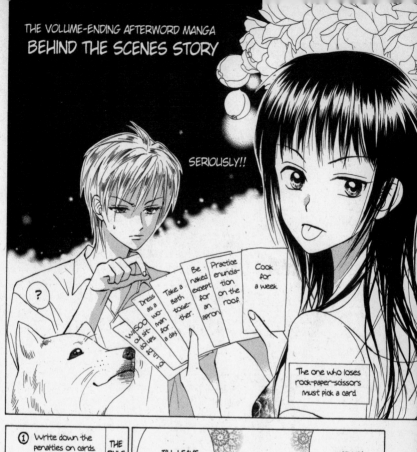

THE VOLUME-ENDING AFTERWORD MANGA

BEHIND THE SCENES STORY

SERIOUSLY!!

?

Cook for a week

Practice enuncia-tion on the roof.

Be naked except for an apron

Take a bath toge-ther.

Dress as a wo-man for a day

500 sit-ups

The one who loses rock-paper-scissors must pick a card

HELLO! FINALLY, WJ HAS MADE IT TO ITS LAST VOLUME.
THE LAST REQUEST WAS "THEIR NEWLYWED DAY." ♪
Pardon me for the silly ideas.
I'LL LEAVE THE RESULT TO YOUR IMAGINATION.
PLEASE TRY IT WITH YOUR FRIENDS, TOO, EVERYONE!
THE RULE.
① Write down the penalties on cards. Note: Never show your partner what you write.
② Do rock-paper-scissors with passion. Note: It must be truly heated.
The cards on which you wrote your penalties will be used together with the ones your partner wrote, so be sure to consider the possibilities beforehand.

If it's a gamble, it's a different matter.

AND...
WHY DON'T THEY HAVE A WEDDING?!
I CAN'T BELIEVE THIS IS THE END.
PLEASE DRAW AN EPISODE ABOUT THEM AS ACTORS!
HOW 'BOUT WJ PART 2?
Part 2?
Their shouts are music to my ears, but...
Ahh.
YES, I HAVE RECEIVED MANY LETTERS LIKE THESE.
BUT I'M SORRY, THE MAIN STORY IS ALL OVER NOW.

IN FACT, WJ WAS SUPPOSED TO END MUCH SOONER.
MY DREAM IS TO DO A TEN-VOLUME SERIES!
It was right around volume 5.
Editor
OKAY, TEN VOLUMES THEN.
BUT WHEN I STARTED TO INCLUDE SUB-CHARACTER STORIES...
IT'S NOT GONNA FIT. CAN I DO SOME MORE?
LIKE 13 VOLUMES!!
You don't have to end it
At around volume 8.

BUT IF I DON'T END IT, I WON'T BE ABLE TO START A NEW ONE!
SUPER SELFISH.

INSTEAD OF DRAGGING THE STORY OUT HALF-HEARTEDLY...
I WANTED TO END IT NICE AND CLEAN.
I settled with 14 volumes in the end
The title will sound weird, too. Maybe it already does.
He's disguising himself as a woman as the penalty from the game.
EVEN THOUGH I COULD NOT DRAW DETAILED SCENES WITH THEM AS ACTORS, THEY ARE HAPPILY LIVING TOGETHER.
BUT...
IT'S TRUE THERE ARE THINGS I ENDED UP LEAVING OUT.
SO...

SOMEDAY, I'LL DRAW A SPECIAL EPISODE!!

WHEN?

THAT... YOU JUST HAVE TO BE PATIENT...

My new series will be my priority.

THAT'S NO GOOD.

ANYHOW, SINCE I COULD NOT DRAW MUCH ABOUT THE SUBCHARACTERS TOWARD THE END...

I WOULD LIKE TO WORK HARD AND EVENTUALLY DRAW THEM ALL.

♫ Yay!
♪ Yay!
PLEASE WAIT PATIENTLY.
JUST DON'T KEEP YOUR HOPES TOO HIGH.
POK
That's not nice!

STARTING WITH THE ONE-SHOT STORY AND INCLUDING THE PREPARATION PERIOD, IT TOOK FIVE AND A HALF YEARS.

WJ AND I ENDED UP WITH QUITE A LONG-TERM RELATIONSHIP.

THE CHARACTERS AND I WOULD LIKE TO EXPRESS OUR HEARTFELT THANKS TO ALL OF YOU WHO CHEERED US ON.

Special Thanks!!

* Y. Shiroumaru
* A. Taneda
* Y. Sano
* R. Fukuyama
* S. Wakamatsu
* A. Oguchi
* R. Fujimoto
* K. Hayashi
* M. Oono
* A. kanno
* Y. Yoneda
* I. Matsuo
* M. Ishii
* Y. Aoki

* Sayaka *

My Family & My dog

Mr. Ando

and you!

Thank you so much for reading through to the end!
By the time this volume is released, my new series should be started. It's a Chinese-style fantasy. I'd love it if you'd read it.
I hope to see you again on pages like these!

2003.2.6. Emura